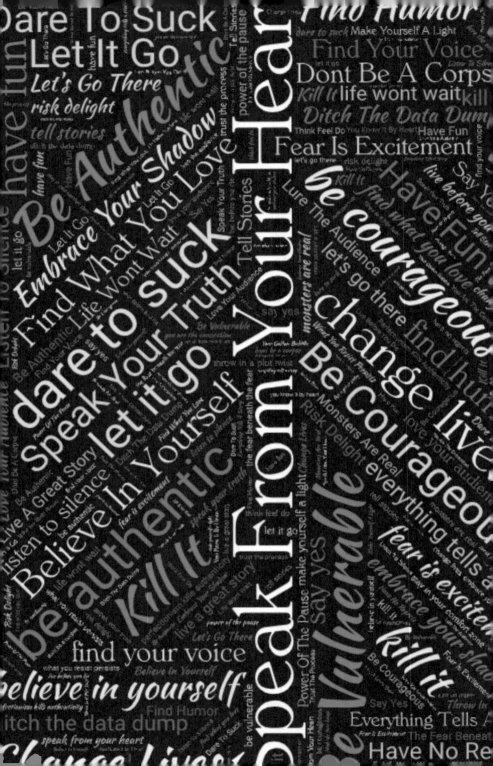

RAVES FOR THE PUBLIC SPEAKING HORROR SHOW 👏

"WOW!!! Laura Reid delivers a MUST-HAVE, MUST-READ, excellent book on public speaking. *The Public Speaking Horror Show* leads you to the other side of your fears and, most importantly, teaches you how to get up, speak up, and own the room... *any* room."

Willie Jones, 1997 World Champion of Public Speaking

"From the deeper reasons behind the common fear of public speaking to practical but powerful tips, Laura shares the wisdom she has collected on her own journey to light the way for others."

Jenny Pentland, Author of *This Will Be Funny Later*

"What is unique and delightful about *The Public Speaking Horror Show* is Laura's darkly funny and entertaining voice. This is one of those non-fiction books that can read like fiction while public speaking fears melt away. Laura has you laughing your way to better communication!"

Mike Carr, 2020 World Champion of Public Speaking, Founder, The Consistency Initiative

"Now and then, a book appears that takes you on a wild and crazy ride with lots of magical twists and turns. Whether you've never stepped onto a stage before or the stage is your second home, Laura's secrets are the key to living an inspired life, sharing your message with the world, and delivering it with your own conviction and magic!"

Paul N. Larsen, MA, CPPC, Founder, Find Your VOICE Coaching Institute

"Many people take the stage, but few own it. Laura Reid's book, *The Public Speaking Horror Show*, teaches you how to avoid the mistakes most presenters make so you can have the impact most presenters don't. If you're ready to own the stage, this book is the gift that keeps on giving to you, your speeches, and your audiences."

Craig Valentine, 1999 World Champion of Public Speaking, Founder, Inner Circle for Speakers

"What a refreshing treat! *The Public Speaking Horror Show's* creative twist on the spooky topic of public speaking will entertain and enlighten you. I strongly recommend reading this book; you'll truly enjoy it."

Jim Cathcart, CSP, CPAE Author of *What To Do When You're The Speaker*

"Usually, I have no patience to sit down and read a book, but *The Public Speaking Horror Show's* unique mix of learning and humor hooks the reader AND delivers valuable lessons."

Mohammed Qahtani, 2015 World Champion of Public Speaking

"This book is fresh, fun, and fabulous. It gives beautiful insights into what holds us back and powerful processes to help you move forward. *The Public Speaking Horror Show's* tips and tricks, interspersed with Laura's hilarious humor, make this book the best friend and speaking coach I know so many are looking for. She will entertain you while also leading you to lean into your fear, uncover your story, and share your voice."

Verity Price, 2021 World Champion of Public Speaking, Accredited Speaker

"If you'd rather be slaughtered by vampires than speak in public, step into Laura's crypt. She'll take you from the graveyard to greatness, from ghastly to gleeful, from ghoulish to... something else that starts with G. Seriously, get this book before the next full moon."

Kevin Burke, 2008 Las Vegas Entertainer of the Year

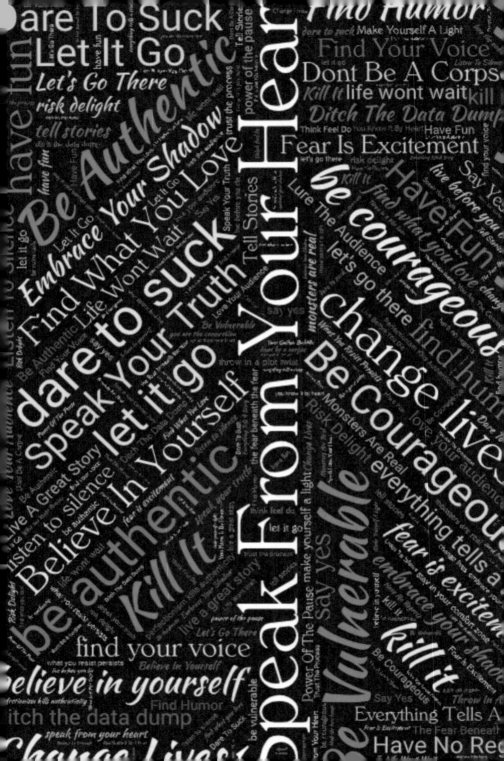

THE
PUBLIC
SPEAKING
HORROR SHOW

7 Secrets to Kill It as a Speaker

Editor: Cain Kamano

Book cover design: Bagsu Teguh Santoso (Saga), *99 Designs*

Back cover portrait & logo design: Elizabeth Stapleton

Inside cover portrait: Ilana Maxwell, *@soulsightartistry*, www.ilanamaxwell.com

Dedication page portrait: Sara Linton, *Sara Marie Photography,* www.saramariehawaii.com

Paperback ISBN: 979-8-9868327-2-2

e-book ISBN: 979-8-9868327-1-5

DEDICATION

For Riley... Once you told me, "Mom, this book is the first good idea you've ever had." 😂 Well, there was one other good idea, YOU. 🖤

Rain or shine... You make me happy.

ABOUT THE AUTHOR

Not peopling today. 😳

Having grown up with a stutter, social anxiety, and an aversion to putting on pants, Laura Reid, M.Ed., is an unlikely international keynote speaker, public speaking coach, and stand-up comic. But that's what makes her uniquely aligned to help others break through public speaking fear and leave audiences spellbound. ✨

Laura has received numerous awards for her speeches and presentations and won several storytelling competitions. She has a penchant for haiku and horror movies. Laura lives somewhere over the rainbow on the Big Island of Hawaii, where she relishes solitude and fends off wild pigs for excitement. 🐗

Did someone gift you this book because you're ready to kill it as a speaker but don't like reading? 🤓 I got you!

Be part of the Speech Slayer community and snag your free mini-course, 👇👇👇👇👇👇👇

"The 7 Deadly Sins of Public Speaking" 🎤🎃

@ www.thespeechslayer.com

No FOMO, 🙆 because you'll be the first to know about upcoming Public Speaking Horror Show masterclasses, webinars, events, and other cool sh*t. 😎

Download if you dare... 🙀

"THE POWER OF CHRIST COMPELS YOU!"
FATHER DAMIEN, *THE EXORCIST*

CONTENTS

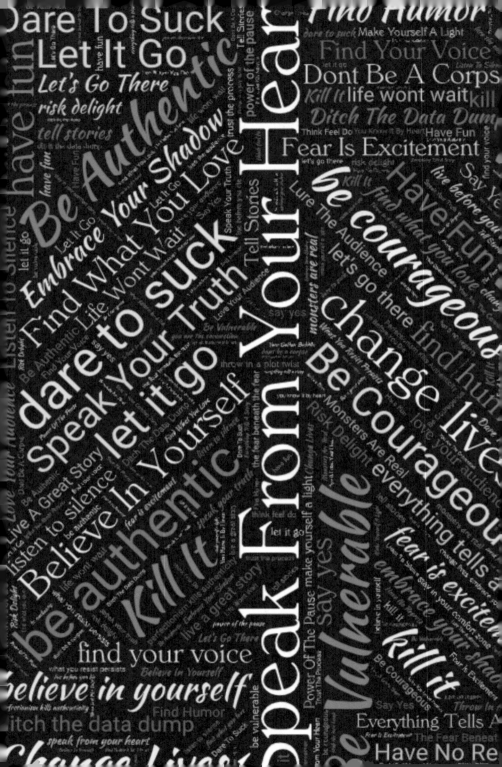

FOREWORD

VERITY PRICE, 2021 WORLD CHAMPION OF PUBLIC SPEAKING, ACCREDITED SPEAKER

When most conversations about public speaking start with the fact that collectively, it is something people fear more than death, you know there's a need. *The Public Speaking Horror Show - 7 Secrets to Kill It as a Speaker*, illuminates the darkness of the fear that is ruling people's lives and forcing them to be silent, take a back seat, and not have permission to shine and share their truth. I was one of those people, and for far too long, I stayed silent. As a teen, my fear was so big that I would fake a temperature by putting a thermometer in hot tea.

By 20, I was convinced that my life was going to be small. But then, unexpectedly, I began songwriting. The words flowed out of me, and with them flowed a dream. A dream that I could step on stage and sing. Unfortunately... my fear followed. Soon, I was caught in a tug-of-war between my dream and my fear. And for years, I let the fear win. I found excuses to not share my songs with people, reasons to not try out for open mic nights, and excuses to *stay* small.

My turning point was losing my father unexpectedly when I was 24. I was suddenly hit with the reality that life is short, and every wasted moment – well, is a waste. I decided to walk across Spain in memory of my dad in 2000, and that 500-mile walk showed me that if I could walk across a country, I could walk onto a stage! When I returned home, I slowly started taking steps towards my dream. I recorded a demo, found a vocal coach, and started stepping onto stages. Within a few years, I discovered that just behind my biggest fear, lay my biggest strength. I loved being on stage. I loved connecting with my audience. I loved sharing my truth.

Because of that, in 2005, I crowdfunded my first album and unwittingly became one of the first people in the world to do so. But as fate would have it, I wasn't destined to be a pop star; instead, my music career unexpectedly led to a speaking one. Because of that, suddenly, I was speaking around the world about innovation and thinking differently and discovered that it was something I enjoyed as much as singing.

That journey led me to Toastmasters, and in 2021, I became the World Champion of Public Speaking. Let me put it this way – the terrified teen me, who was putting thermometers in hot tea to **get out of** speaking, would never have believed that speaking would become my life.

And do you know what would have helped me conquer my fear and find my voice that much quicker back then? A book like the one you are about to read. A book that could take the horror show out of speaking to reveal the confident speaker within you.

I would have given anything to have Laura's quick-witted humor and sage advice in my pocket. To have been able to reflect on my fears, jot them down, and slowly give them a voice, so that I could reclaim mine. It would have been a godsend to read her journey of finding her voice and to realize that I was not alone in facing my fears.

This book is fresh, fun, and fabulous. It gives beautiful insights into what holds us back and powerful processes to help you move forward. The Public Speaking Horror Show's tips and tricks, interspersed with Laura's hilarious humor, make this book the best friend and speaking coach I know so many people are looking for. She will entertain you while also leading you to lean into your fear, uncover your story, and share your voice.

Here's to this book being all you need to kill it as a speaker and slay self-doubt and fear.

Yours in speaking up,

Verity

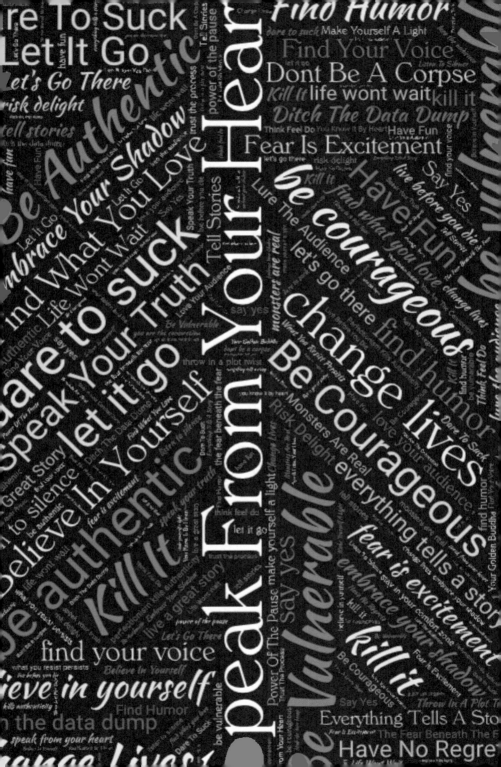

A WORD OF WARNING

" WORDS HAVE NO POWER TO IMPRESS THE
MIND WITHOUT THE EXQUISITE HORROR OF
THEIR REALITY.

— EDGAR ALLEN POE

*D*ear Brave Soul,

Proceed with caution. This book will crack you open and let your guts spill out.

It's not for the faint of heart, squeamish, or timid soul.

Nevertheless, if you possess a sense of urgency to show up for yourself, conquer what's been holding you back, and share your unique voice, story, and brilliant ideas with the world, then grab your dagger 🗡 and come with me.

This book is not meant to be gently held. It's meant to be scribbled in, highlighted, and underlined. Go on, take out your pencil, or dare I say, Sharpie, and mark up the pages with your insights, ideas, and inspirations. If a bit of metaphorical blood spills onto the pages 🩸 let it remind you that you're still alive, and you have purpose.

A little splatter is expected when we allow ourselves to be vulnerable. One day you'll make your final exit. May you do so with no regrets. If you're fearful with nerves, it simply means... it's time to be brave.

Remember this - all the courage you'll ever need is already within you. All you have to do is believe it's there. Belief emerges out of action. It doesn't matter how small or significant the step is. As you read these words, you're already taking action toward believing in your courage.

The root of "courage" is COR, the Latin word for heart. ♥ 🫀 Speak from your heart, and your courage will emerge, with every beat, until your last.

But fear not, Brave Soul, for it will all work out in the end... 😉

I have endless admiration for everything you already are and all that you'll become.

Go kill it,

xo, L. 💋

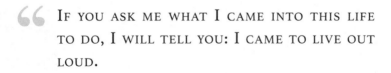

> IF YOU ASK ME WHAT I CAME INTO THIS LIFE
> TO DO, I WILL TELL YOU: I CAME TO LIVE OUT
> LOUD.
>
> — ÉMILE ZOLA

PROLOGUE
A GHOST STORY

> " MONSTERS ARE REAL, AND GHOSTS ARE REAL
> TOO. THEY LIVE INSIDE US, AND SOMETIMES,
> THEY WIN.
>
> — STEPHEN KING

~

a ghost in the night
repeating my name, Laura
this is not a dream

~

Do you believe in ghosts?

One night, around 2 AM, when I was six, I awoke to the sound of the heater in my bedroom rattling, as if the temperature had suddenly dropped.

I turned over in bed and saw a girl staring at me. Her eyes were like a dead fish. Murky, watercolor eyes. My body froze; my heart boomed in my ears.

Then I had the most terrifying realization - *this is not a dream.*

The only movement I dared was to blink... she was still there. Then she began to sing. Her song was only one word. She repeated it as she walked alongside my bed, "*Laura... Laura.*"

Even though it's been decades, that night still haunts me.

It's believed that what we give our energy to will expand and grow.

But what if we give all our energy to fear?

As a child, I didn't know why I saw that ghost, but it makes more sense today. I grew up with a severe stutter that made speaking nearly impossible. For reasons I'll never understand, my name was the hardest thing to say. Because of that, I became deeply ashamed and developed social anxiety and a paralyzing fear of public speaking. I felt like a coward, terrified to be asked the most simple question, "What's your name?"

As I grew up, I learned how to hide who I was, and because of that, I began to believe I was worse than a coward... I was a fraud. The amount of effort it took to get through a networking event, job interview, or even a staff meeting without an anxiety attack was exhausting. That exhaustion and anxiety became normal for me. Eventually, instead of healing what was asking to be healed, I turned to a quick fix, anxiety medication. Although the medication helped numb my anxiety, it dampened something less easily defined. It was as if a part of what made me, me... was sacrificed. And interestingly, I was ok with that; I was ok with not being me.

Hiding who I was and being *unseen* became my superpower; in fact, I became so skilled at it... I became like a ghost.

When You See a Sign, Follow It

Now I'm not sure precisely who you are or why you're here... but if you've ever hesitated to step into the spotlight, speak your truth and share your stories, you should know that confidence can be just around the corner.

Because one day, I discovered the most unlikely place of refuge...

A stage and a microphone.

How did I get up on that stage? I walked. 😉

(Did I mention I'm also a stand-up comic? It's still a work in progress. 😂)

I don't know if you've ever felt this way, but there was this sudden sense of urgency. I could either take the risk of facing my greatest fear or accept the alternative... continue living in shame and regret.

In the Spring of 2012, I walked past a flyer for a story-telling competition. I don't know what made me notice it, or why I stopped and stared at it. But looking back today, I believe it was a sign from a higher source; in this case, it was a literal sign. And it appeared to me when I was meant to see it. Then, without even thinking about it, I knew what to do. I entered the contest.

Have you ever had moments like that? Where it was the scariest thing you'd ever done, but leaning into that fear changed everything?

I can now see how that moment, reading that flyer, led me to be where I live today, doing the work I do, and finding true love.

I'll never forget that feeling of not only being on stage but of how many people came up to me afterward, congratulating me on winning the contest and, more importantly, what my story meant to them. I've been on many stages since, and that's still the most thrilling part for me - getting to know that what I shared was meaningful and helpful to someone.

Here's the thing, when you speak and share your voice and story, you MAY feel vulnerable, and it CAN be scary, but when you're in the act of it and aligned with your message, there's nothing to fear.

You become a conduit. You're not only connecting.

You ARE the connection. ⚡

WHAT YOU SEEK IS SEEKING YOU.

— RUMI

I believe this book has been seeking you, and I'm thrilled you found it.

My intent for this book is to empower you to **kill it as a speaker** and never become like a ghost. Well, until, you know...

I WOULD LIKE, IF I MAY, TO TAKE YOU ON A STRANGE JOURNEY.

— THE ROCKY HORROR PICTURE
SHOW

SECRET ONE

WHAT YOU FEAR WILL SET YOU FREE

66 THE CAVE YOU FEAR TO ENTER HOLDS THE
TREASURE YOU SEEK.

— JOSEPH CAMPBELL

∾

darkness approaches
it tugs you near, embrace fear
treasures await you

∾

I Knew I Had to Make a Change

∾

I had just gotten a new job as a Montessori teacher in Ithaca, New York. I'll never forget sitting in my first teacher training and reading the word on the agenda I feared most:

INTRODUCTIONS. 😱

The other teachers began to go around the room and introduce themselves with ease. But as it got closer and closer to my turn to speak, I felt a flush of anxiety wash over me. Then nausea, followed by shortness of breath. I didn't know it then, but I was having a full-blown panic attack. I knew I wouldn't be able to say my name... that I would be "found out." Everyone would laugh at me. I was back at school again, not as a 42-year-old teacher, but as a little girl who just wanted to fit in.

I ran to the bathroom, eventually went home "sick."

I was more ashamed, humiliated, and embarrassed than sick, but that day, I knew I had to make a change. It would be years later before I eventually followed my fear up onto a stage and told my story. But since then, the most profound lesson I learned was that **what I feared would set me free.** And it set me free in ways I never could have imagined. I went from being unable to introduce myself to a small group of teachers to being an international keynote speaker, speaking coach, and even stand-up comic. (The most terrifying speaking of all, but also the MOST freeing!)

What would it feel like to be free from your speaking fears and let that freedom lead you beyond your wildest speaking dreams? I believe it's possible for you. Whether you realize it or not, reading this book shows that you believe in yourself; continue to do so. Because places and stages are waiting for you... Get ready.

What Are You Afraid Of?

No, but for real, why is public speaking so scary?

I used to say it's not like anyone has ever died from public speaking, but I stopped after my friend told me he knew someone who had a heart attack behind a podium 😲. Still, it's rare... like getting attacked by a shark. Actually, I know someone who... never mind, let's move on. The point is, it shouldn't be as scary as it is, but it is... why?

When it comes to fears, what are you afraid of? Most of us are scared of something: 🕷 spiders, heights, clowns 🤡 another Zoom meeting 😵 . Some fears might be improbable, like a global pandemic; what are the odds? 😷 Wait... never mind. 🧑‍🦰

Yet the National Institute of Mental Health cites that public speaking remains one of our most common fears among more than half the population. 🙀 (Is it just me, how is it not clowns... hasn't anyone else seen *IT*? 🎈)

We usually won't get physically hurt unless we fall (or jump) off the stage. Still, we collectively fear speaking even more than DEATH! Why?

I believe it's because we see death as inevitable and public speaking, as a choice. But what if we viewed it like death... inevitable?

You see, even a hermit living alone in a cabin in the woods eventually has to venture into town for supplies and talk to people. There's no escaping public speaking.

The scientific word for fear of public speaking is "glossophobia." Although it sounds more like the fear of too much lipgloss, 👄 it comes from the Greek words "glossa" (tongue) and "Phobos" (dread or fear).

The word "dread" describes a future fear. That's good news. It buys you time.

Because if you're willing to put in the work to ponder and consider what you're truly afraid of and where that might lead, then today's dread could be tomorrow's delight.

The Fear Beneath the Fear

There's a good chance your speaking fears are the same as many others. I spent years being scared of the little girl on the side of my bed coming back. Eventually, I saw her as a metaphor. Initially, I thought I was afraid of saying my name because of my stutter. But eventually, I learned it wasn't the ghost or my name; what I dreaded most was the fear beneath the fear:

☞ Embarrassment

☞ Shame

☞ Humiliation

☞ Judgment

And these fears grew to:

☞ Lack of confidence

☞ Self-doubt

☞ Depression

☞ Desire for isolation and solitude

☞ Few friends

I've found writing down what I'm afraid of, makes the fear less scary. In a minute, you'll be doing the same. (Cue the theme from JAWS.🎵🎵) 🦈

What You Resist, Persists

Have you heard of the saying, "What you resist, persists?" The idea is from Swiss psychiatrist Carl Jung, who wrote that "what we resist, not only persists, but will grow in size." Think about that. Your fears will set you free, but only if you embrace them and dare to stare them down. (More of this will be covered in Secret Four, "Your Shadow-Self Needs a Hug.")

Fear is like an illness you want to cure, but first, you must identify your symptoms. 🙂

When you're hurt or sick and ignore, put off, or resist medical care, your symptoms and/or illness will likely be there tomorrow, the next day, and the next. Unless you die, then they'll go away. 😉

But going to a doctor is at least a productive step, like hiring a plumber if your sink is leaking or a speaking coach if you have a speech coming up (shameless plug, but hey, it's my book, so... 👻) But when it comes to the fear of public speaking, most people tend to want a quick fix, but that's like putting a bandaid on a severed head.

We may tell ourselves, "If I ignore it, it will go away." But instead, what we ignore festers. It *persists*. When fear persists, it grows, demands our energy, drains us of positivity, and eventually, it might consume us. Why do we let it persist? It could be because it's easier to do nothing than to do something. Taking no action takes little effort. Identifying our fears might be challenging, but action without clarity or purpose is tragic. I've tried the *ignore it, and it will go away* method with everything from a mole, social anxiety, and an ex-husband, but it simply doesn't work that way. One way to make something different from what it is is to face it and take action.

The same is true regarding our nervousness and fear about speaking. The more we can pinpoint our speaking fears, the better we can move forward with actions to free ourselves from them.

So, when it comes to public speaking, *what are you afraid of?*

Write your fears in a word or sentence below:

I'm not sure what fears you wrote down, but these are the top five public speaking fears my clients have shared with me:

1. Judgement 😬

2. Making mistakes 😣

3. Forgetting words 🫠

4. Being boring 😴

5. Embarrassment 😳

Whatever **your** fears, accept them because acceptance is the opposite of resistance. Look at it this way, when you welcome and appreciate your fears, you acknowledge your whole self instead of ignoring the vulnerable parts that could become strengths. For example...

Your symptoms might hold the secret to the cure...

1. If you fear **judgment**, it could be telling you to **let go of other people's opinions** or to work on **building your self-esteem.** Wise words I've heard and repeat to myself often are, "Other people's opinions are none of my business." And here's the game-changing knowledge I wish I'd known decades ago: *no one is thinking about you.* When we're in the audience, we're primarily focused on *WIIFM* (**W**hat's **I**n **I**t **F**or **M**e). There isn't space in our heads to think about when you misspoke or forgot your words or when your PowerPoint slides

didn't work perfectly. Why waste your time worrying about your mistakes when no one else is? It sounds a little harsh, but doesn't it feel wonderful to know that no one is thinking about you? Yipeeeeeeee... 🤸🤸🤸

2. If you fear **making mistakes,** your fear could be telling you to **let go of perfection or join an improv class!** Public speaking is not an arena that applauds polished perfection because authenticity has far more power. Perfection kills authenticity. Let it go, and you'll feel free to take the stage with a renewed dedication to be your most authentic self. 🦄

3. Regarding the fear of **forgetting your words,** the remedy may be simple, **practice.** Put in the time and effort to build your confidence. Then, you can focus on feeling your words rather than telling them. Instead of memorizing every word, paint a picture in your mind of what segment comes next and then allow yourself flexibility. Free yourself from having to say every word "perfectly." Remember that the audience has no idea what you plan to say and will only know when you make a mistake if you tell them! By the way, never tell them. 🦉

4. If you're worried about **being boring, ask yourself, "On a scale of 1-10, how passionate am I about this topic?"** If it's low, then what would it take for it to be 10? How can you spin it to make it more exciting? Do you have an amusing story to add? A well-told story is never

dull. Remember, if you're bored, there's an excellent chance your audience will be too. Ask yourself how you can have fun and get excited about giving your presentation. If you're having fun, the audience will too. Consider bringing in props, creating colorful slides, disrupt the status quo! Allow yourself to be bold and try new creative ways to get your message and point across. Your audience will thank you for it.

5. If one of your fears is that you'll be **embarrassed**, your fear may be telling you not to **take yourself too seriously.** Remember that life is a stage! Sometimes, you might be called to play the jester; sometimes, you may be the hero; other times, the villain. But no matter what part you play, if you approach it with joy and a lightness of heart, any embarrassment you feel will quickly fade.

Today, when I see the word "INTRODUCTIONS" on the agenda, I can't wait to say, "I'm Laura, and I'm happy to be here." (And mean it.)

〜

    " IF FEAR CANNOT BE ARTICULATED, IT CANNOT BE CONQUERED.

— STEPHEN KING

There's no wrong answer, and your answers might change over time. But this gives you a starting place for what you want to work on. Ultimately, remember that each of your fears will set you free.

Write below what your fears or symptoms might be telling you...

~

DO YOU HAVE THE COURAGE TO BRING FORTH THIS WORK? THE TREASURES THAT ARE HIDDEN INSIDE YOU ARE HOPING YOU WILL SAY YES.

— JACK GILBERT

Say "Yes," not only so you can discover your treasure but also to be able to give it away to those who need to receive it - those whose lives you'll change.

When you say "yes," - the following could be you...

"I've never spoken publicly before and could never do what you do." One of my clients didn't think she could speak in front of an audience, but she hired me anyway because she sensed she could no longer leave her story untold. We began our work by digging up her story, and it was immediately clear to me that her story had a message that could change lives. I helped her apply to speak at an international conference, and she was accepted. "OMG! You're IN!" I was so excited for her, but she was less enthusiastic, "OMG, I'm terrified," she said. I knew something she didn't yet; I knew that this fear would set her free and that her story would impact others in profoundly positive ways she couldn't yet see. How could she? But then, on the day she spoke, she began to understand. She called me right after her presentation, crying, and said five words I'll never forget, "You just changed my life."

She not only killed it as a speaker and slayed that day, but she also received the coveted "Best Presentation" award. From there, her life began to change in ways she never would've anticipated. It's only been a few years, but since then, she's given numerous award-winning speeches and become a best-selling author, podcast host, TV show host, and successful business coach and trainer.

She went from never speaking to always saying *yes*.

> THERE IS NO GREATER AGONY THAN BEARING AN UNTOLD STORY INSIDE YOU.
>
> — MAYA ANGELOU

What untold story awaits? It's time to set it free.

SECRET TWO
SLAY IN YOUR COMFORT ZONE

    " L<small>IFE</small> BEGINS AT THE END OF YOUR COMFORT ZONE.

                            — A LOT OF PEOPLE

I disagree.

I prefer to stay
in my comfort zone, I slay
my mind remains calm

*W*hen I was a child I was told I was shy. *I wasn't really.* When I was a teenager, I was called a loner. *I couldn't fit in, so I stopped trying.* As an adult, I'm called an introvert. *Absolutely accurate, 💯%*

In my comfort zone with my favorite horror
movie pillows. Also wine.

I Think I'll Stay In, Thanks

It's hard to go a day without reading or being told in some way to get out of your comfort zone. It's as if our comfort zones are an uninhabitable planet where nothing grows. Therefore, if you never step outside your comfort zone, your life will amount to a little more than a pile of... comfy pillows? I don't know about YOU, but my comfort zone is MAGNIFICENT. And yes has an unreasonable amount of comfy throw pillows because, as a great philosopher never but should have said, "The amount of happiness in one's life can be measured by the number of pillows they are surrounded by." 😊

At its MOST extreme, as an adult (here's where you and I may differ... especially if you're an extrovert), my true comfort zone relies on an absence of people. That void is instead replaced with pajamas, fuzzy blankets, books, old copies of *The New Yorker*, and possibly a jar of Nutella and a spoon. Awwww, just writing that makes my soul feel cozy.

When I was younger, my comfort zone was also anywhere people weren't. Being around other people made me primarily uncomfortable because they would expect me to talk. And then, when I couldn't speak, they would be confused, and I'd feel embarrassed and judged, and then shame would reliably set in, and I'd wish I was alone, back again in my comfort zone. *I think*

I'll stay in, thanks! That taught me that getting out of my comfort zone was not fun.

Still, I heeded the ubiquitous warnings and advice and forced myself out of my comfort zone. And in so doing, in many ways, it helped me grow, learn and achieve more. Sometimes however, it only taught me that I can scream MUCH LOUDER than I ever thought possible. Like that time, I got WAY out of my comfort zone, and (insert word here: courageously, recklessly, stupidly) bungee jumped from 111 meters high over the Zambezi River. I remember thinking, "WHAT ARE YOU DOING! ARE YOU CRAZY? ABORT ABORT ABORT."

IKR? I could do THIS, but was terrified of speaking? 😱

The funny thing is, stepping out on a stage for the first time wasn't much different than stepping off that plank. I jumped. I screamed. And by the grace of God, I didn't die. 🙏

But stepping (or screaming) out of my comfort zone came at a considerable cost when it came to public speaking. I would put a lot of pressure on myself to be confident and self-assured, even though that wasn't how I felt. I would lean into the familiar refrain, "Fake it until you make it." Because of that, I became the opposite of authentic.

Strangely enough, sometimes I could pull it off.

Mainly because the only real goal was to GET THROUGH it.

Have you ever told yourself that you just need to "get through it," and THEN you'll be OK? I feel you. When we focus on only getting to the end result, we miss out on the power of being present. And to be an engaging speaker, you must be a present speaker.

Early on, speaking was nothing more than a linear process for me. I would coach myself to silently spit out one word after another until I reached the end. Point A to Point B.

Point A was terrifying, and the path to Point B was filled with landmines, traps, and obstacles, but if I raced as fast as I could, I might make it to the end. And only then could I breathe... and often, collapse at the finish line. That process, at least for me, was exhausting. And only validates and perpetuates feelings of dread. Yet I'd still reward myself because CONGRATULATIONS, I got out of my comfort zone!

Brain Freeze

Consider this, when your brain notices that you're about it get out of your comfort zone, it responds accordingly. Your brain says, "OH HELL NO!" And promptly pushes the "RED ALERT" button triggering all the appropriate responses for imminent fear: sweat, shaking, twisting stomach, dry mouth... and the worst of all when it comes to speaking... forgetting words you once knew by heart when you were back in your comfort zone. Brains are smart like that.

Now, I'm not a brain scientist, but I believe this is an accurate depiction of what your brain looks like when you tell yourself you're getting out of your comfort zone.

Your brain outside your comfort zone.

It's like drinking a smoothie too fast and getting a brain freeze, but without the health benefits of a smoothie.

Has that ever happened to you? You've rehearsed and rehearsed and know what you want to say, and when you practice in the shower or in front of your mirror, you totally crush it. I mean, you're GOOOOD!

But then suddenly, when you're in front of an audience, you can't seem to remember your own name, you stumble on your words, and it's as if your brain froze... and not in the kind of way when you drink that smoothie too fast... it just stopped working.

Your brain is only trying to help. It means well. And you can't blame your brain for having a response meant to protect you.

After all, you told yourself you were about to "get out of your comfort zone," right? Face your fears and all? Jump off that metaphorical cliff? Well, guess what, your brain heard you... it *always* hears you.

I've found there's a much better way... it's the opposite of getting out of your comfort zone, which, you guessed it, means staying IN it.

I'm curious, where's **YOUR** comfort zone? On a mountain, in the ocean, in bed, under blankets?

The question is, how do you *FEEL* when you're in your comfort zone?

Write down the words that come to mind below...

Now, ponder what you wrote. Is there any fear, dread, or nervousness there?

I predict that some of your words might include: peaceful, calm, myself, relaxed...and maybe...going out on a limb here... COMFORTABLE? 💀

Have you ever worried about remembering what you wanted to say while you were in your comfort zone? I'm going to guess no. Although I often need to remember where I put the TV remote.

When it comes to your comfort zone, YOU have the ability to warp reality in YOUR favor.

You have the power to remain "comfortable" even when you step away from your couch, put on pants (oh, the horrors!), and venture bravely into the deep, dark, spooky woods, a.k.a., any speaking situation not taking place on your couch.

Consider this... what if you could **STAY** in your comfort zone, even in *uncomfortable* situations?

After some trial and error, I learned it's possible. But the really cool discovery was that I still experienced all the change and growth that I thought happened only *outside* my comfort zone.

It Worked

Right before you speak, set a clear intention... visualize yourself IN your comfort zone feeling "relaxed, calm, yourself..." all your most loved comfort zone feelings while delivering your presentation.

It will be as much of a game changer for you as it was for me. For example, last month, I spoke at a conference. Right before I went on stage, I set an intention to feel peaceful, grounded, and present, as I do when I'm at home with my comfy pillows on my couch. It worked. I took that feeling onstage with me, and each time I do this, I feel more and more present, confident, and connected.

Knowing I could stay IN my comfort zone while doing something scary changed my life.

I began to accept more invitations to do terrifying things, like attending networking events and speaking on more stages. I knew that I could metaphorically be sprawled out on my inner couch; instead of FREAKING OUT...

I was SPEAKING OUT...

unafraid, empowered, and COMFORTABLE!

My brain was like, "Wait, what just happened? Where's

the brain freeze? Where's the panic, anxiety, and dread?"

Your brain in your comfort zone.

It was such a new and unfamiliar sensation it almost seemed too good to be true. But it wasn't. I had somehow tricked my brain and body into believing what I was about to do would be fun and relaxing, and I had nothing to fear!

When The Moment Comes

I recently spoke at a women's leadership conference in Ashland, Oregon. It was one of the largest audiences to date I'd spoken to, and I was getting a bit nervous. Still, I reminded myself to silently step into my comfort zone. I felt the grounded, inner peace I feel when I'm on my couch with my JAWS and The Twins from The Shining Throw pillows. I felt this sense of no expectations. I didn't put any pressure on myself. Instead, I trusted in the belief that I could remain in my comfort zone. And guess what? It was one of the best presentations I've given to date, based on the standing ovation and feed-back I received. It would've gone much differently if I hadn't first grounded myself in my comfort zone. I stepped into the light, and I was finally able to shine. No exhaustion, no anxiety or dread... just pure light.

And when the moment comes for you to step into that light, you won't be stepping out of your comfort zone.

You'll **step into it.**

SECRET THREE
YOUR VIRTUAL HELLSCAPE TELLS A STORY

" COMPUTERS ARE LIKE OLD TESTAMENT GODS; LOTS OF RULES AND NO MERCY.

— JOSEPH CAMPBELL

~

zoom zoom zoom zoom zoom
social distancing prevails
forgot to unmute

~

What Could Possibly Go Wrong?

On March 3rd, my 53rd birthday, I boarded a plane from Hawaii to Indonesia. Knowing I would be speaking abroad for the first time at a women's leadership conference felt like one of the best gifts ever. I was optimistic and excited; I was about to achieve my goal of becoming an international keynote speaker! And on top of that, I had just won my first Toastmasters International Speech Contest, which meant I'd be progressing to the next level.

What could possibly go wrong? 😁

The answer to that, I'd soon find out, was a GLOBAL PANDEMIC. Good one, Universe. Did NOT see that coming.

Thankfully, before the world nearly ended, I did give my keynote presentation, not yet realizing it would be the last in-person speaking gig I'd have for the next two years.

It was equally impossible to predict that, apparently, planes don't fly during a pandemic unless you've got your own private jet. And Jeff Bezos wasn't returning my calls.

At home in the rice field, 🌴 Ubud, Bali

Consequently, I spent 123 days away from my family; in a remote rice field in Ubud, Bali, living with two men from Serbia, both named Vladimir. But THAT'S a book for another day. Stay tuned...

What I'll share though, because I love a good story, I eventually referred to the Vladimirs as "My Vlads." They became the brothers I never knew I needed. We all experienced a profound transformation over our shared quarantine and have matching dragonfly tattoos to prove it!

Dragonflies in the rice field tattoos, me and My Vlads. Ubud, 2020

The Tiny Dot

The good news was I'd still get to compete in the next level of the Toastmasters contest. The bad news was it would now be virtual. And in my case, I'd be competing from Ubud. The time difference was NOT in my favor. Although groggy, I remember it all well...

It's 3 AM.

I'm standing where I'd marked my bedroom floor with tape, feeling ridiculous in a white suit and red lipstick. I stare at my laptop screen and begin to SILENTLY FREAK OUT.

It was so dark I had rounded up all the lamps in our house and pointed them at my face. When I went to plug in one of the lamps, I received an electric shock - but I was so nervous that all I could think was it could only help. I prayed for no earthquakes or thunderstorms, like the night before, no loud feral cats yowling outside my window, no snakes outside my door, and most of all, I prayed for a strong wifi signal, zoom connection, and working microphone.

Despite my trepidation, time moved forward, and then suddenly, it was my turn to speak. That's when the out-of-body experience took hold, and I relied on pure muscle memory of my mouth to say the words I had practiced repeatedly. I stared so hard into the tiny dot at the top of my laptop screen that I was pretty sure I looked crosseyed to the virtual audience. The number on the Zoom screen told me that I was speaking to over a hundred people, but that seemed hard to believe. Mostly I felt like a crazy woman in a white suit talking to no one.

I was incredibly relieved when it was over, and I didn't pass out or start yelling profanities 🤬 into the screen. I turned off my video, muted myself, and plopped onto my bed to happily watch the other contestants sweat it out. I thought I had a good chance of winning, but one contestant stood out. He was engaging and charismatic, and I knew I could learn much from him. Within a few seconds of his speech, I knew he would win.

And I was right; he took first, and I took second place. I was also right about learning a lot from him because a few years later, he became my fiancé. Win-win.

The Virtual World

Following the contest, it became clear that all my future speaking opportunities would be virtual too. That meant I had to learn how to excel quickly in the virtual world.

And that's what I did. I learned. I tried new things and observed and made mistakes. Eventually, someone noticed that I was pretty good at speaking virtually, and asked me to give a workshop. Since then, I still collect tips and techniques to continue to improve and help others present the best virtual webinar, talk, workshop, speech, or any other goal they have.

Post-Pandemic World

Now it's 2023, and we're in a post-pandemic world. But Zoom and virtual speaking still prevail. Sometimes I still feel stuck in a virtual Hellscape. I mean, even Zoom is sick of Zoom; I just updated it on my computer, and a screen popped up that said, "Go meet in person!" 🤣

But all joking aside, speaking virtually can be incredibly effective and engaging. For one thing, everyone has a front-row seat!

Over the past few years of virtual speaking, here's what I've learned...

Everything Tells a Story

When I was young, I loved to go for walks in cemeteries. 🪦 I assume most might find this creepy, but I found it peaceful. There was a quiet order and an absence of clutter. I'd read the names, dates, and epitaphs and wondered about the lives of those buried beneath. I couldn't help but create stories in my mind based on what I was seeing.

What do cemeteries have to do with virtual speaking?

No matter what we're looking at, a cemetery or a zoom background, everything tells a story.

When it comes to virtual speaking, the questions to ask yourself are:

"What story do you *want* to tell?" And, "Are you telling that story?"

What do you notice when you open Zoom or begin recording a video? What stands out? What needs improving?

If you own a business and have a brand, is your background in line with that?

For example, if your business is decluttering homes, but your backdrop is cluttered, the story you may be telling is not supporting your brand.

Not all stories are told by speaking or reading; visual storytelling is ubiquitous.

Remember, you're telling a story when speaking virtually, whether you planned to or not. It's better to control your own narrative.

Here's how... **Lights, Camera, Action!** 🎬

There's a reason this is every director's mantra. Lighting, camera, and action can be either a disaster or a triumph when speaking virtually.

Let's start with lighting...

Don't Be a Corpse

Buddha said, "Make of yourself a light."

OK, so he wasn't talking about ring lights, but the essence of his message applies, *light yourself up!*

Essentially, don't be a corpse. 💀💀 Your lighting is telling a story, don't let the story be a dark one.

Any photographer knows this essential truth - never underestimate the power of good lighting. Lighting was not something we had to think about before the zoompocolyse. But now, it's an everyday thing. Again, everything tells a story. And in this case, the story is your face. If your face is darkened and we can't even see your expressions - a story is being told, and it might not be flattering.

Here's how to fix this; it's easy-peasy, and if you want to look like a movie star, it can cost anywhere from nothing to under a hundred dollars. Place your computer or laptop screen in front of a window so the light shines towards you. Your face will be beautifully lit if you're speaking during the day.

Beware of too much overhead lighting, as that can drown out your features, and you'll look ghostly. I love that look, but most humans will find it... chilling.

When I was in the speech contest in Ubud, natural light was not possible because it was 3 AM, and I had no access to computer light accessories. Thankfully, one of My Vlads helped me gather all the lamps we could find, and we placed them behind my computer screen shining light towards my face. We unplugged lights behind me, so I was only dimly backlit, and the effect was amazing! Using lamps around your house can create a similar result for zero cost!

In my home, I love the look of the windows in my bedroom and wanted that as a backdrop. But when light is behind you, your face becomes silhouetted. My solution - order a ring light. I now have a portable ring light on a tripod for under fifty dollars, and I'm impressed with the results. Even when speaking at night, the light casts a very flattering, soft glow onto my face.

So you now have a few solutions to look like something other than a corpse. No excuses!

HORROR SHOW ZOOM PRO-TIP

Check out the current video settings in Zoom, and if you dig deep enough, you're likely to find "studio effects." Here you can "correct your appearance," LOL, which basically smooths out your skin tone. At the time of this writing, you can even pick and choose from a variety of eyebrow and lipstick filters! Just don't learn the hard way as I did that if you happen to be drinking from a white coffee cup, your lovely red lip filter will jump right off your lips and land on the cup! True story. Never again.

Everyone Has A Front Row Seat

It's been said that the eyes are the windows to the soul; not making eye contact during a virtual speech is like hanging dark curtains in those windows.

So, first things first, be sure to know where to look. Locate the tiny camera lens on your computer, laptop, or phone. Next, practice looking directly into the lens. Now, practice speaking while keeping good eye contact as if you're talking to a friend. Eye contact is as crucial as ever and, in some ways, even easier. Your audience is right there, on the other side of your lens.

Remember that it's OK to break eye contact now and then. But just like in a live speech, if the speaker looks down *too* often to read their script, it creates a disconnect. In most virtual meetings I attend, even though most of us have been on Zoom for a while now, some people still speak directly to the Brady Bunch boxes instead of looking into their camera lenses... probably because they don't know better. (Consider sending them a copy of this book? Another shameless plug.)

Once you've nailed looking into the camera, get your camera height right. This might mean stacking boxes, books or buying a tripod. But honestly, you can find ANYTHING on the internet; I love my desk riser thingy (official name, btw) that I place on my regular desk when I'm giving a virtual talk. While there are many ways to set your camera angle, play around and find what works best for you. It might depend on how close or far away you are. I prefer to have the camera lens right above my head and tilted slightly down; I'm typically, whether sitting or standing, about three feet away from my lens.

Ultimately, regardless of the angle, distance, or height, please get to know where that lens is; it's the most essential part of your virtual speaking. Consider it a portal from you to a beautiful big stage in front of a captivated audience.

Remember, when you're speaking virtually, *everyone* has a front-row seat!

HORROR SHOW VIRTUAL EYE CONTACT PRO-TIP

Stick up a photo of a loved one or a sticky note with an arrow next to your lens. This will remind you not only to look towards it but may also make you smile more. I like to stick a little picture of my son next to the lens to remind me to speak from my heart and of one of the reasons I do what I do.

Pro-tip example

The Blob

OK, here's the deal. Virtual backdrops can be cool, but please test them out. Sometimes if the person speaking moves even a bit, it suddenly looks like they are being consumed by The Blob! (1958 horror movie, stay with me people!) The best thing to do is test your background first to ensure you won't scare anyone, unintentionally. A green screen can help, just like in Hollywood; it helps bring your backdrop to life with added clarity. Word of caution, unless you'd like your head to appear severed, don't wear green with your green screen. 🩶

Also, a simple, plain bookshelf works well as a backdrop. Be selective as to what you put on it and allow for plenty of empty space. Pick items that again, tell the story that you want to be told. For example, in my background, I often speak in front of my desk and have in view my typewriter (yes, I still use it). And if I'm feeling not so humble, I'll have a few speaking trophies in sight too. The point is, I have items that are meaningful to me but also tell a story that I'm a writer and a speaker. And a bit old school.

My current virtual… but real background.

HORROR SHOW BACKDROP PRO-TIP

Quick declutter solution…

Hang a curtain behind you to instantly create an elegant backdrop. Don't tell anyone, but I have some plush red velvet drapes that I use as a backdrop for speech contests, so it looks like I'm on an actual stage, or at least I have an elegant home. But in truth, they're hiding a huge mess - our guest bed, which also doubles as a place to stack papers that likely will never end up in an actual file.

Uplighting effects…

An affordable way to create a dramatic effect, especially if you hang dark curtains behind you, is to have lamps out of view but with their light directed towards the sides or up from the floor so it creates an excellent spotlight effect. This effect will appear more dramatic if you turn off overhead lights.

Ditch The Data Dump

I once worked with a group of scientists to help them make their presentations more engaging. One of the scientists wanted to give a presentation on an algorithm he helped design. His initial approach was lots of information and data packed onto PowerPoint slides. At the end of the workshop, he decided to ditch the data dump and instead begin with a story of the algorithm! It began, "Once, there was an algorithm...." He led us through the journey of its creation, and we were all spellbound! He proved that any seemingly dry or overly scientific topic can be made into a compelling story.

Remember that your slides are there to ENHANCE your words, not BE your words.

Sure, it may be easier on YOU to have your entire presentation and script on your PowerPoint slides and scroll through and read them. Still, your audience may think what I tend to think when I have to sit through that kind of presentation, "This could've been in an email." 🧑

The other old adage is also true, "a picture is worth a thousand words."

Use compelling photos and illustrations whenever possible. Get personal, don't shy away from real images. Suppose you tell us about the time in high school when you knew you had found your purpose in life to become a photographer after being in the yearbook club. In that case, we'll wanna see photos... show us that mullet!

Another tip is to increase the font size when you have words on your slides. And remember, fewer words are better... we can read faster than you can speak, so if you're reading most of your presentation from the slides, we're already done.

Consider this fabulous advice, the 10-20-30 rule, from author, speaker, and marketing guru Guy Kawasaki. It states that for a great presentation, have 10 slides, speak for only 20 minutes, and you should have at least a 30-point font.

Lastly, leaving your audience wanting more is a good thing.

Your intention is to generate interest, give your audience a delicious taste of your topic, idea, or business, and not force-feed them the whole nine-course meal.

Just remember, when creating your slides, they also tell a story. Ask yourself with each slide if it's necessary and enhances the presentation. If it doesn't, DITCH IT.

For The Love of All Things Holy

If you're giving a formal virtual presentation, do this one simple thing, for the love of all things Holy, STAND. I realize we've all grown even lazier as a species, but consider standing if you're giving a speech or presentation 10 minutes or longer. The exception would be an interview or panel discussion where the host or interviewer is sitting. Otherwise, stand. Not only will you look much more professional and allow your hand gestures to be seen, but it will also improve your breathing and voice and help to your calm nerves. Be sure though, to stand firmly in place unless you are leaning in to make a point, and not give in to the temptation to sway or move unnecessarily. Taking a step or two to the side is OK, but when speaking virtually, the most effective use of your "stage" is to lean, or move, in closer.

Keep your hand gestures in the frame and only use them to emphasize a point.

Above all, remember to OWN IT. Own your space, feel grounded on the floor, and no matter what, have fun.

While there's been a common refrain that it's impossible to have the same kind of connection virtually that we do live, this may not necessarily be true. Just because it's different doesn't mean it's bad or wrong.

People can still feel a deep connection to your words and message. If YOU do, THEY will.

And let me state again, lest you forget - everyone has a front-row seat! Make the most of that fact and never "phone it in" to "get through it" and wait for better days. First of all, those days might not ever come. Secondly, take advantage of the opportunities and benefits of speaking virtually and reaching people all around the world. The virtual possibilities are infinite! Well, of course, depending on your Zoom plan.

～

SECRET FOUR
DIG UP YOUR BURIED STORY

" YOU EITHER WALK INSIDE YOUR STORY AND OWN IT, OR YOU STAND OUTSIDE YOUR STORY AND STRUGGLE FOR YOUR WORTHINESS.

— BRENÉ BROWN

~

authenticity
the story you hide within
a survival guide

~

*I*t's time to ***dig up your buried story.*** This will be fun, I promise. So grab your shovel, and I'll meet you out at the cemetery. See, I told you, FUN.

Frightening Fun Fact:

Nothing is more powerful than the story you don't want to tell.

Find, Follow and Flow

Find

How do you find your most impactful stories?

To start, it would help if you went deeper and darker, not wider and lighter. Run towards the darkness, not away. I know it sounds scary. That's because it is. Embracing your darkest and/or most painful memories goes against the general cultural and societal assumption that positive thoughts are what we ought to lean into. But you wouldn't be reading this book if you weren't ready to go THERE. Right?

What are some of the experiences in your life that brought you to your knees? What made you cry unexpectedly or question your beliefs? What embarrassed you so much that your face still turns red when you think about it? **Let's go *there.***

A few decades ago, I was in a writing workshop. It was in the workshop instructor's old historic townhouse outside Washington, DC. I still remember sitting on pillows on the creaky wood floors as he gave us writing prompts. Then we'd go around the circle sharing what we wrote and offering feedback. One prompt asked us to find a news headline from a few local papers and use it to inspire a story. One headline that stood out to me made my stomach turn over. It read: "Women Killed by Thrown Cement Block While Driving to Work."

At that time, I commuted to work daily from Alexandria, Virginia, to Washington, DC. On the way to work, I was usually mindlessly singing along to the radio or worrying about what the day might bring at my office job. Often on the drive, you'd go under bridges; sometimes, people looked down at you from a spot on the bridge. I wouldn't think much of it. Maybe this woman was also lost in her thoughts, but on *that* day, when she drove under the bridge, a few kids decided to throw a cement block over. She died instantly. Had she left a few seconds earlier or later, she might still be alive today.

That news story still haunts me occasionally when I'm driving. Yet, it seemed too dark and raw and tragic. I wanted to write about her, what her morning was like, and then contrast it with the events that led to the boys on the bridge finding the cement block. The workshop leader saw me hesitating and asked if I'd chosen a story. I eyed another headline about the opening of a new library and then said, "Well, a part of me wants to write about the death of this woman while she drove to work, but I guess because I drive to work every day too, I don't want to go there."

He looked me in the eye and said,

"*There* is exactly where you need to go."

I'll never forget that. Whenever someone says, "I don't want to go there," I think of that advice and repeat it to them. Sometimes I get a funny look back, probably similar to the look I gave him then. Yet that advice has served me well when it comes to telling my story and finding stories that'll have the most significant emotional impact. If we only tell happy, positive, shiny stories, we aren't having an effect other than passing the time. And as I will keep reminding you, whether you want me to or not, time is not something to let pass because we never know when it will run out. Just ask the lady driving to work that day who made the papers.

Follow

Here's why you need to go *there*. We must follow those stories that touch, scare, and inspire us. The stories that create an **emotional connection** in you are bound to do the same in others. And that emotional connection is CRUCIAL.

What makes it all the more challenging is that our most powerful stories have often been kept in the dark for years.

They've been collecting dust and cobwebs for so long that they're barely visible and almost forgotten. We've hidden them because they made us feel... uncomfortable, unsettled, and vulnerable. Historically, humans don't like that feeling. With that said, some stories might not be ready to tell; trust yourself to know the ones that must be told and the ones you can keep buried.

Flow

Once you have found your fears and followed them to the stories they have led to... it's time to allow for the FLOW. The flow is your internal floodgates opening. It's the expansive, boundless bounty of your creativity unleashed. It's innately imperfect, even a bit chaotic, yet gold can be found in all that vast mess.

To be in the flow means to begin the dirty work of getting words onto paper. My gifted artist dad told me, "Don't wait for inspiration; you'll be waiting until you're dead, DO THE WORK, and inspiration will find YOU."

The only way to get in the flow of creating is to begin. You'll know when you're in it. You'll feel it. And it won't be perfect, and that's the goal. You are STRIVING for IMPERFECTION! Perfection kills creativity. That's worth repeating; say it with me, write it down on a sticky note, and stick it to your mirror to remind you, PERFECTION KILLS CREATIVITY.

When you're in the flow, it will feel effortless. I believe when aligned with our stories, passions, and truths... our words will flow. It doesn't mean that we won't have to work hard to get our hard work out into the world; it simply means that we won't need to swim upstream to get there. And the beautiful thing is, when we create from that place of flow, we can deliver from that place too, and our audiences will more quickly receive our message. Flow happens from within but also from an elevated state. From that perspective, life is a bit easier; the breeze blows, time slows, and our words flow.

What I feared most was speaking in front of an audience. That fear was easy to find because it had been with me my whole life. Yet something compelled me to follow that fear. Listen to those "somethings." Those often tiny tugs telling us to take notice. Look for the signs. Follow them to find your story. When you do, you will not be **in** the flow; you *will be* the flow.

Intermission Story-time: The Golden Buddha

I came across this story on Wikipedia, so it must be true. 😉

There once was an enormous statue of Buddha. Although its size was impressive, no one paid much attention to it as it was made of clay and had little value. Then one day in 1955, a group of monks moved the statue from one temple in Thailand to another. But the Buddha was much heavier than they thought. When the monks attempted to lift it from its pedestal, the ropes broke, and the statue crashed to the ground.

Because of that, layers of plaster cracked open, and gold illuminated from beneath, to the monk's astonishment. The monks worked with hammers and chisels until the entire statue was revealed to be made entirely of pure gold.

No one knew that several hundred years earlier, an attack by the Burmese army was imminent. More than anything, the Thai monks of that time wanted to protect the golden Buddha from being destroyed by the army. They covered it in layers of clay to conceal its value. All of the monks died in the attack. The Buddha survived, but its secret was lost until a single crack unearthed the truth.

Your Golden Buddha is Your Story

Over time, you may pile layer upon layer of clay over your Golden Buddha.

You may suffer from the weight of your limited beliefs, self-doubt, inaction, and inner critic. You know - the constantly cranky voice in your head telling you that you're not worthy enough, smart enough, thin enough, rich enough... on and on. I've got one response to that... enough!

The other layers of clay get added on from external influences - social media overload, stress, financial pressures, comparison to others' success... gluten. LOL!

Eventually, you may be so laden with clay that you forget that gold is even there. And worse, you may believe the outer layers define you. You may spend years, or in my case, decades, masking your truth.

But right now's the time, in this very moment, to embrace and empower that light illuminating from our inner gold. That light, your golden Buddha, is *your story*.

Face to Face

It was hot. Bangkok hot. I was with a group of other speakers at a conference touring temples. I didn't know it then, but I would find out later that the enormous, golden Buddha I "randomly" sat across from and prayed face to face... was THE ACTUAL Golden Buddha from the story. It was my birthday. And I asked the Buddha for courage. At the time it took up all the courage I had to speak at that conference, I knew I still had layers to shed. The thing about shedding layers is that everything you're searching for is already there, within you.

. . .

Shedding the layers helps you see it more clearly, but faith teaches you to see even in the dark.

The actual Golden Buddha, March 3, 2019

The Day I Owned My Story

The room was noisy and packed. The host of the story competition called my name, and suddenly the microphone was before me, and I held on for my life knowing this was the day I owned my story. I believed that if I didn't finally speak my truth, the weight of my layers of clay and shame would bury me alive.

The story I told that night:

When I was a little girl, my hair was so long it fell past my waist. My mother would braid it and pin the braids on each side into giant loops. A toddler could swing from my hair.

Then, when I was nine, my parents divorced. Because my mother began drinking and could no longer care for me, I eventually went to live with my Dad and new Stepmother, Ellen. Ellen made me get my haircut so short everyone thought I was a boy. I don't know if I'll ever understand why she despised me; I was only a child. But I've come to believe that maybe it was because something about me and how much my dad loved me brought out something hurtful in her. And hurt people hurt people. My hair was one small, seemingly benign way she could hurt me. There were other, more obvious ways, but her control over my appearance was easy for her to validate as "normal."

I never stood up for myself. I never said, "I don't want to get my haircut." Instead, I surrendered to the monster living in my throat. When I tried to speak, it ate my words. Sometimes I didn't mind because it was easier to stay quiet. Most of the time, my stutter was my enemy, but sometimes it was my friend.

But as I got older, my appearance began to matter more to me. With my severely short bangs and boyish cut, I didn't like my reflection. But worse, I didn't like who I was on the inside either; I was a coward.

Then one day, something remarkable happened. Ellen got sick. Because of that, she neglected to make my haircut appointment for a few months. My hair began to grow. I looked in the mirror and smiled.

Eventually, Ellen got better and resumed making my appointments.

But on the day of my next appointment, something within me shifted. My slightly longer hair gave me the slightest whisper of confidence. But just enough to give me the courage I needed.

On that day of my haircut appointment, I got off my school bus, went inside, and walked straight to the object I feared most in our house, the telephone.

Now in those days, phones were ENORMOUS and sometimes attached to the wall! My fingers were sweaty, and my hands shook so much it was hard to dial. I kept having to start over.

But then, I got through. Regina, the owner of Reggies Hair Salon, answered the phone, it was the hardest thing I'd done, not only the speaking, but because I knew the consequences would be harsh. But I did it.

"...I w-w-w-w-want to c-c-c-ancel m-m-m-my ap-p-p-p-ointment!"

The strain it took to force the words out past the monster made me yell them and breathe heavily.

There was a long pause, and Regina said, "It's OK, darling. You can reschedule."

At dinner that night, I sat across from Ellen, and she stared at my hair. Then she asked a question to which she knew the answer: "Laura, did you go to your haircut appointment today?" I stared down at my spaghetti and shook my head.

Another long pause, and then, "That's OK, I'll cut your hair tonight."

That night, while I was in my room, I heard her call my name. I came to the top of the staircase. She stood at the bottom, gripping a pair of shiny scissors.

I descended the stairs because I didn't have a choice; I was a child.

Then I heard my dad's voice. He said, "You are not cutting my daughter's hair."

Later, my dad told me I had given him courage that night. I had never thought of myself as brave before.

My voice, courage, and hair grew a little more that day.

～

I did it. I told my story out loud. The next time I heard my name called was when they announced the winner.

And just like that, I stopped struggling for my worthiness.

You Know It By Heart

Stories are part of our human DNA.

Have you ever listened to someone tell a story, and suddenly it's as if you're in the story yourself? Stories can create empathy. Because of that, they're a catalyst for change. Remember that your story might give someone else permission to share theirs, which might change their life. Therefore, not sharing is not only holding you back; it might be the very thing someone else needs to hear.

When you share a personal story that's meaningful to you, there's nothing to fear because it comes from the heart and - you know it by heart.

Your Brain On Stories

When we listen to another person share a story, our brains light up in a way that no other form of communication can match. Scientists have discovered that "feel good" chemicals like cortisol, dopamine, and oxytocin are released in the brain when we hear a story. These are the neurochemicals associated with empathy, creating deeper connections with others, increased memory, and a sense of emotional connection to the storyteller.

I'm not a brain scientist, but this is your brain on stories, and it's... adorable?

Completely accurate rendering of your brain on stories.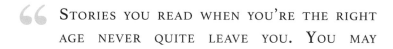

> STORIES YOU READ WHEN YOU'RE THE RIGHT
> AGE NEVER QUITE LEAVE YOU. YOU MAY

FORGET WHO WROTE THEM OR WHAT THE STORY WAS CALLED. SOMETIMES, YOU'LL FORGET PRECISELY WHAT HAPPENED, BUT IF A STORY TOUCHES YOU IT WILL STAY WITH YOU, HAUNTING THE PLACES IN YOUR MIND THAT WE RARELY VISIT.

— NEIL GAIMAN

Let's visit *those* places.

Your Shadow Self Needs a Hug

YOUR VISIONS WILL BECOME CLEAR ONLY WHEN YOU CAN LOOK INTO YOUR OWN HEART. WHO LOOKS OUTSIDE, DREAMS, WHO LOOKS INSIDE, AWAKES.

— CARL JUNG

We often consider vulnerability a weakness, yet it's one of our greatest strengths as speakers.

Sometimes audiences can sense when a speaker is being disingenuous. Vulnerability takes courage and a deep acceptance of who you are- the good, the bad, and the OMG NO! But what does vulnerability have to do with your shadow?

One of the bravest things we can do is unearth the darkest parts of ourselves that we've kept buried and hidden from others.

Ironically, a potent speaking tool is already within you. There is one tool in particular that, when resurrected, will give you more courage and confidence than anything else combined. That tool is what the Swiss psychologist Carl Jung referred to as your shadow. He believed that *"everyone carries a shadow, and the less it is embodied in the individual's conscious life, the blacker and denser it is."*

You may recall from Secret One, "What you resist persists." Therefore, when you stop resisting and EMBRACE your shadow, you'll feel lighter, more at ease, and more confident. When you approach a microphone, you'll do so without the weight of fear, for once you unite with your shadow, you're no longer resisting. Imagine what it would be like without fear of judgment, mistakes, or doubting yourself.

Your shadow embodies all the negative traits you fear someone will see in you; we often work hard, as I did, to hide this part of ourselves from the world. But once you accept your shadow self and even bond with it, there is nothing you can't do because you have nothing to hide. And that's my definition of vulnerability.

The following practice was adapted from the brilliant book, "The Tools," by psychiatrist Phil Stutz and psychotherapist Barry Michels. They were inspired by Carl Jung's shadow-self research and developed tools to help people overcome fears and build confidence.

I've found it to be incredibly effective for everything from getting in touch with your story to overcoming stage fright. So if you dare, it's time to meet your shadow. Because your shadow self needs a hug.

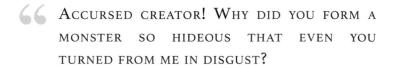 ACCURSED CREATOR! WHY DID YOU FORM A MONSTER SO HIDEOUS THAT EVEN YOU TURNED FROM ME IN DISGUST?

— MARY SHELLEY, *FRANKENSTEIN*

Meet Your Shadow

Take a deep breath in your nose and out your mouth three times.

Now, think about and write your answer to the question on the next page:

What about myself am I ashamed of and hide from others?

~

The feelings this evokes might be uncomfortable, but push the feelings forward and give them a living form.

What you see is unique to you. It might be monster-like more than human. It might be a child or an older person, and it might even be an animal.

Sketch out your shadow below...

Meet Your Shadow: The Sequel

I invite you to *speak directly to your shadow* and ask:

"What do you need?"

Write your shadow's response below:

~

Finally, tell your shadow:

❤ "I love you."

❤ "I accept you."

❤ "You are safe."

Continue to do this activity periodically and notice how your shadow changes. Doing the activity as a visualization practice during meditation might be helpful.

The first time I saw my shadow, it was a big, grey blob. I realized that's how I see myself at my worst, like a mass of nothingness. As a child, I also imagined a monster-like blob living in my throat that would eat my words when I tried to speak.

But after I began the shadow work, the blob became a little girl. It was me as a child, and I was alone and scared. When I asked her what she needed, she said, "To be heard." I told her she was loved, accepted, safe, and heard. This practice was a total game-changer with my courage and confidence. Now, when I imagine she's there with me on stage, SHE'S HAPPY.

I've done this exercise with numerous clients; their shadows have emerged as everything from a rabid dog to a caged goddess. But the common denominator is the immediate feeling of liberation. As if something buried is suddenly set free.

Every time you speak publicly and notice nerves emerging, take a moment to close your eyes and tell your shadow that it's loved, accepted, and safe. Allow your shadow to be right on stage with you; together, you have nothing to fear.

Your shadow not only helps you ACCEPT your story, but it can also help you find the stories that have the most meaning for you.

Begin making a list of stories that come to mind that hold meaning to you, and then find a message within the story that would have meaning for an audience.

Then to help you draft and develop your initial stories, here's a bare-bones 💀 approach I conceived to classic storytelling: The S.C.A.R.E.© storytelling model. 🔪🧟

The Horror Show Storytelling Model: S.C.A.R.E.©

S 💧 SCENE - Set the scene by bringing your audience into the *room where it happened* (nerdy *Hamilton* reference 😌). Add visual and sensory elements so they feel like they're there. Bringing them into the scene grounds them in a place and time and helps them begin to picture the setting you've painted for them. For example, *"It was early morning; I walked onto the stage and immediately felt the gaze of hundreds of eyes. My dad had tied my tie too tight. And since there was no A/C, the audito-*

rium felt like being in a furnace. I was only 12, and being a contestant in the National Spelling Bee was about to change my life forever." The audience has enough information in just three sentences to create a picture.

C ◆ CONFLICT - Introducing conflict or conflicting forces after the setting raises the tension and keeps the audience in suspense. The audience already knows the scene, but uncertainty and stakes begin to build when adding conflict. For example, continuing with the spelling bee story above, you could add the following sentence: *"Just then, as I walked up to the microphone, I noticed a face in the second row of the theatre. Not just any face, but the face of Big Bad Bradley Becker. The bully who had shoved me into my locker the day before, and I wondered, What was he doing there?"*

A ◆ ANGUISH - I hate to be the bringer of bad news, but for a good story to work, some sh*t has to go down. And things will likely go from bad to worse. 😬 That's where anguish comes in, encouraging the audience to empathize with our main character. (There's a reason why so many Disney movies begin with the protagonist becoming an orphan. Think Bambi.😭) Keeping with our poor spelling bee contestant, here's how adding anguish might look: *"There was something sinister about his smile. I wished it was my mother in the audience instead of him, but no amount of wishing could've cured her cancer and brought her back. I gripped the microphone tightly and* *tried to focus on the moderator as he introduced me. But something caught my eye; Bradley was discreetly holding up a sign with a single word, I couldn't quite make it out, but it looked like "LOSER." I instantly thought of all the times he taunted me, even on the day my mom died, "Loser, loser, loser..." The judges said my name, and I knew I was only seconds away from knowing my word and fate. A bead of sweat ran down my face.*

R 🔵 REVELATION - OK, a little relief now, 😁. Revelation gives the main character/hero sudden, surprising wisdom, courage, or strength to challenge the conflict. After your audience fully invests in your hero's fate, the revelation grants them relief and permission to celebrate in your hero's victory. Let's look at how that might play out for our speller. By the way, I'm making this story up as I go, so I'm in a bit of suspense myself! 😅

"Then I remembered my glasses were in my front suit pocket. And all of a sudden, I was the one with the sinister smile. The word on Bradley's sign actually read, "LOOSER." I couldn't believe it; Big Bad Bradley Becker was dumber than I thought. And just then, I realized the sign was a SIGN. After all, I was the one on stage, and he was such a loser that he couldn't even spell it. At that moment, I knew I had nothing left to fear. The moderator asked if I was ready. I had never been more prepared. Then I received my word, "PNEUMONIA." I couldn't believe it; that was a cinch, espe-

cially because I had just recovered from pneumonia over winter break. I began to speak, "P-N-E-U-M-O-N-I-A."

E 💧 **EPITAPH** - In this case, the epitaph is the final message for the audience. It solidifies that the hero has gained new knowledge or skills that'll potentially change their life. So good news, our speller is gonna be OK. Most likely. 🌙🙏

"'Grandpa, tell us how it ends!' I looked down at my great-granddaughter and said, "Well, if you want to know if I went home with the biggest trophy that night, I did. But the real prize was knowing I had the courage, confidence, and belief in myself even while a bully was staring me down and trying to throw me off.' She smiled up at me and put her tiny hand in mine. It wouldn't be long now. The hospital machines were beeping out a last song. I was ready to go; at 88, I had lived much longer than expected. And I couldn't help but admire the irony of my demise. I was dying from pneumonia." (The end.) Sorry, but I never promised a happy ending. 😊

There are numerous storytelling frameworks, structures, and models out there for you to explore. Find what works for you and have fun with it.

The good news is I'll share one of my favorite go-to frameworks in the next chapter! 🤓

SECRET FIVE
(WITCH)CRAFTING YOUR SPEECH

> " A WORD IS DEAD ONCE IT IS SAID SOME SAY. I
> SAY IT BEGINS TO LIVE THAT DAY.
>
> — EMILY DICKINSON

buried in my head
blank screen and dread, stuck again.
put words on paper.

Your words are spells. Cast them well.

Seven Steps For Getting Your Presentation Out of Your Head and Onto Paper

*B*eing prepared means different things to different people. I prefer to write out my entire speech, work my way down to an outline, and ultimately be practiced enough for the delivery that I can ditch the script.

Although there are many ways to prepare, if you're new to writing speeches, I highly suggest writing out your entire script word for word. Why?... writing it out will help you spot errors and redundancies, know the word count, see the scope, arc, and layout of your speech, and enables you to choose your words with economy and precision.

When we write down our words, it also helps us to remember them. Getting your ideas out of your head and down on paper is a process most (if not all) professionals rely on to achieve the best possible outcome. If writing it out sounds like nails on a chalkboard, consider using a transcription program like Otter or another speech-to-text app. The benefit of speaking out your script is that your speech will naturally have your own conversational tone.

If you want to be clear, concise, and stay on point, winging it is your LAST option. Yet sometimes, while helpful, even a simple outline can feel daunting. So where do you start?

The following steps will help you keep your momentum in crafting your speech; putting the work in, however grueling, will pay off. Pinky promise.

Step One: What's Your Message?

Your message unlocks the treasure chest for the audience. Make sure the key fits. 🔑

Even if you've been assigned a presentation or repeatedly present weekly (like a Monday morning meeting) or already know your topic or key takeaways, you can keep it fresh. For example, suppose you work for a hospital presenting new medical research or giving a financial update to stockholders, or you're a tech CEO presenting the latest and greatest upgrades. In that case, there's still an opportunity to go deeper than what's assigned and deliver a well-thought-out message every time.

A speech or presentation without a clear message for the audience is like handing someone a beautifully wrapped present 🎁 that's empty inside (ouch). It might look pretty outside, but it could leave your audience disappointed and confused.

So how do we formulate our message?

An excellent place to begin is with the "Think, Feel, or Do" model...

Think, Feel, Do

1. What do I want my audience to *think (know or understand)*?

Is there a mindset change, idea, or a bit of wisdom you want your audience to take away from your speech? For example, in one of my recent speeches, I used one of the messages from this book, "what you fear will set you free." I wanted the audience to think differently about fear and how it can lead to unexpected breakthroughs. While fear has been a topic of thousands of discussions, keep in mind your perspective (and your personal stories) on the topic is what matters. Provide your unique take and own your expertise.

2. OR... What do I want my audience to *feel*?

Maya Angelou said, "People will forget what you did, they will forget what you said, but they will never forget how you made them feel." Do you want your audience to feel inspired, motivated, loved, or appreciated? Write that feeling down in the margins as you craft your speech. And once you hone in on the feeling you want them to have, you can more clearly decide on the content and stories that'll evoke those feelings.

3. OR... What do I want my audience to *do*?

A speech without a call to action is often a missed opportunity. So what is it that you want them to do? Buy your product? Use your services? Practice self-love? For instance, if you want your audience to practice more self-love, you may want them to take out their phones and schedule a time that week to do something that brings them joy.

HORROR SHOW MESSAGE WRITING PRO-TIP

Keep in mind that your message is like the foundation of a house. Without it, everything you say falls apart.

How do you make your foundation strong?

I love this tip from The 1999 World Champion of Public Speaking, Craig Valentine, who suggests using fewer than ten words when crafting your message. Why? Because the fewer words in your message, the higher the likelihood it will be more evident to your audience. And as Craig Valentine also says, "A confused mind says no, a clear mind says go."

Why This Topic Now?

You'll be closer to finding your message once you've answered one of the three questions above. But keep in mind your topic and your message, while they could be closely related, are different. A topic is more broad, and your message is specific. Your topic might be "How to Get Away with Murder," but your message could be "Everyone's Innocent Until Proven Guilty."

Once you've decided on your topic and message, it's worthwhile to ask yourself, "Why this topic now?" Because here's the thing, behind every "Why" is a story.

So, what's the story? To give you an idea, I gave a speech in 2021 entitled "Answer the Call." The topic was "regret," but the message was about appreciating loved ones. I chose it because I didn't want others to experience the regret I felt by not answering the phone when my dad had called a few days before he died.

Being clear on MY why helps me have more conviction in delivering my message. Being clear in YOUR why may help you do the same.

Being clear and concise is harder than it seems... It takes patience, practice, and time. In fact, I think this well-known author said it best:

> 66 I DIDN'T HAVE TIME TO WRITE YOU A SHORT LETTER SO I WROTE YOU A LONG ONE INSTEAD.
>
> — MARK TWAIN

So let's practice. Here's an exercise to get you going...

If you need help with a concise message beyond the Think/Feel/Do model, write down answers to the following questions in ten words or less. Make it quotable!

✍If you had the world's attention for one minute, what would you say?

~

What are the top three life lessons you've learned?

If you knew you'd die tomorrow, what's the number one message you'd want to pass on to a loved one?

HORROR SHOW LIFE-COACHY PRO-TIP

Notice that you're NOT asking yourself:

Am I qualified to deliver this message?

Remember, you're an expert on your story and experiences.

Why should I deliver this message when someone else can do it better?

Just because Brené Brown speaks brilliantly about vulnerability doesn't mean you don't have your unique take and wisdom to share on that topic. I mean, about EVERY topic in the world has already been talked about; some people may have had all kinds of degrees and certifications, and some don't; it doesn't matter. You can hear the same message from a hundred speakers and not get it or have it inspire you until, for mysterious reasons, one speaker delivers it in a way that finally hits you.

Step Two: Who's Out There? Know Thy Audience

It was my first-day teaching as a Peace Corps Volunteer at Mapombo Secondary School in Mudzi, Zimbabwe.

My first lesson would be on the meaning of cultures mixed with a bit of world geography. I rehearsed, over and over, an eloquent introduction about where I had traveled from and how, for all the differences in our homes and cultures, there were many similarities too.

As I stood before my classroom and gave my lesson, my students appeared mesmerized.

I'm crushing this, I thought.

When I finished my beautifully delivered introduction, I paused to ask if there were any questions. A girl in the back raised her hand. I was thrilled; questions already! That was always a good sign that I had stoked their curiosity.

I called on her to speak, and she smiled and said politely, "Madame, we don't speak English."

As a clueless young teacher in Zimbabwe.
Luckily, my students taught me well.

Although my trainers told me that most of my students would be fluent in English, I learned that day that it's essential to do your own research and never make assumptions. Learn as much as you can about your audience, and they'll appreciate you for it, or at the very least, they'll understand what you're saying!

Every Audience Is Different

It was my first all-women stand-up comedy performance at a 490-seat theatre, and it was packed, well, packed for "Covid." There may have been 80. And check this out; the first few rows were CARDBOARD CUTOUTS of people (sh*t got WEIRD during the pandemic 🌑).

It felt incredible when my jokes landed, and the theater filled with laughter; I mean, even the cardboard cutouts were laughing. I was riding a high after that, so I decided to do the same set when I was booked for a stand-up gig the following week at a bar. Why not? I thought it killed at the theatre; why wouldn't it do the same for drunk people?

Comics talk about "bombing," and I always thought it mostly meant that not all the jokes landed; maybe there

was some awkward silence. After that night, I understood that bombing is worse than that... It combines
humiliation with these existential questions: "Why do I
exist?" "What's the meaning of life?" and "Who
decided the alphabet was in alphabetical order?"

Nevertheless, it was one of my best learning experiences on stage. 🙏

~

At the time, I needed to grasp the importance of
performing for different audiences at different venues. I
remember feeling so annoyed that the bar audience was
talking, drinking, and not paying attention. But that wasn't
on them. It was on me. The other comics at the bar that
night seemed off the cuff. They bantered with the audience, their sets did not come off polished or rehearsed,
and they killed. They understood the "who," and I'd over-
looked them, even though they were right in front of me.
Ultimately, here's what you need to remember... every
audience is different, know which one you're talking to.

Here's the thing, don't be afraid to suck. Because one
thing you can count on is... at times, you will. Put yourself in front of as many different audiences as possible.
Sometimes you'll kill it; sometimes you'll bomb. But
each time, you'll begin to suck less. 😶

HORROR SHOW FOCUS ON THE WHO PRO-TIP

If you're giving a workshop, breakout, or keynote, ask the event planner for the sign-up list beforehand, so you'll get an idea of the demographic you're speaking to. In fact, ask them as many questions about the audience as possible without annoying them... or sounding creepy... or sketchy... or stalky... nobody likes a stalker.

HORROR SHOW LIFE COACHY PRO-TIP

Never blame your audience. No matter the size or demographic, no matter what kind of day you're having, if they aren't laughing at your jokes or following your directions or even if they're heckling you... always love your audience. It's the greatest gift you can give.

Step Three: The Opening - Lure The Audience In

My dad was a great storyteller. He looked like Santa Claus in an Indiana Jones hat.

He'd tell me stories about adventures with his cousins, about his favorite books and poems... and about heartbreak... when he and Mom divorced.

My favorite childhood memories are fishing with him in our little wooden row boat. I was in charge of baiting the hook with the worm, and my dad was in charge of the donuts.

He taught me that love is like fishing; it takes a lot of patience... *and a little bit of luck*. And if you're unlucky in love, well... *there's always donuts.* 🎣🍩

On the way to the lake, we'd pick up worms at this little bait shop. They sold them in the same styrofoam cups as the coffee, which may have caused confusion and a few unlucky patrons thinking they were about to take a sip of Morning Joe and instead got a cupful of Morning WTF.

Once in the rowboat, I'd open the Cup O' Worms and dig in my fingers to pull one out. These were thick, fat, squirmy earthworms with surprising fortitude and strength. Some were so long I couldn't fit all of it on the hook, so I'd rip it in two and stuff the other still wiggly half back into the cup.

Once cast out into the lake, the worms served a superior purpose, their sacrifice not in vain. They became... The Lure.

~

No lure, no fish. No fish, and you're in for a long, boring sit in a boat.

The same goes for a speech; no lure, and the audience is in for a long, boring sit in their seats.

The lure's purpose is to hook your audience in, set the tone for the speech or presentation, and give them a hint of your key message.

Because of that, *the first few moments of your speech are the most important.*

Make your lure enticing, and your audience will trust, appreciate, and maybe even love you for it. 🤭

Here are some of my favorite ways to lure your audience in... 🐟

Four Ways to Slay the Opening

1. Begin with a question.

When you ask your audience a question, even if it's rhetorical, it can instantly pull them in, generates curiosity, and encourages engagement.

Keep your questions related to your key message and pose them in an intriguing way.

Here are some prompts to help you get started:

- What if...?
- Have you ever thought...?
- How would you feel...?
- When was the last time...?

2. Begin with an interesting fact, statistic, or number.

Sure, the adage is true, "facts tell, stories sell," but beginning with a statistic or startling number related to your key message will leave your audience wanting to know more. Extra points for having the number or percentage blown up big on your slide for emphasis or a photograph representing your statistic to hook the audience further.

I once began a comedy set about suicide, anxiety, and depression (you know, the funny topics 🐵) this way:

"1-800-273-8255, that's the suicide prevention hotline. I memorized it... Why I'm sharing this with you is... just in case my set goes REALLY bad... but so far, I'm killing it."

What do you think? Do you want to know more? If so, my lure set in. 🎣

3. Begin with a quote.

A go-to way to introduce your key message while hooking your audience in is with a quote. I love to begin with quotes because someone more brilliant and famous than me already came up with the perfect words to express my theme.

When I speak about finding your voice and story, my personal go-to is Rumi,

"What you seek is seeking you."

When you find quotes that inspire you, copy and paste them into a file on your computer so you'll have some to choose from when you're ready.

4. Begin with a story.

Launching right into a story or anecdote will lure your audience in while prolonging the suspense. Humans are hard-wired for stories, so a story can be one of the most effective ways to grab their attention. (Unless your audiences are zombies or tax collectors, in which case, please don't audit me.) Beginning with a story is my fave. I find it the most reliable way to gain an emotional connection with your audience and to introduce your message.

So I just gave you four ways to open a speech, but there are dozens! You could open with a magic trick, sing a song, dance, eat fire 🔥... the sky's not the limit; it's only the beginning. 🪂

HORROR SHOW OPENING PRO-TIPS

☞ Be like a tree. 🌳 Remain grounded, and don't move around at the start of your speech. It's better to start with the audience focusing on your words, so don't distract them by walking around and making a lot of gestures in the opening. Imagine having roots growing out from the soles of your feet and planting you right where you stand. After your opening, it's OK to unroot yourself.

☞ DON'T begin by introducing yourself and telling your audience what you'll be talking about... why? Because it's boring and basic. Repeat after me: "I don't do BASIC." 💅

☞ Starting with words like "Picture this" or "Imagine" are reliably engaging prompts for your audience.

 DRAMA IS LIFE WITH THE DULL BITS CUT OUT.

— ALFRED HITCHCOCK

Step Four: Build the Body - Tell Stories

Build the Body:

So you've got an enticing opening; your audience is lured; now what?

The purpose of the body of your speech is to support your key message and introduce comprehensive points to elaborate on your topic, all while keeping your audience engaged. Interestingly enough, you can support your message by using some or all of the same ways to open your speech (Quotes, questions, anecdotes, etc.)

Depending on the length of your speech or presentation, creating an outline is an easy way to begin building the body. Think of it like a house; if your message is the foundation, the outline is the framework. The stronger the framework, the better the house will hold up (even in a zombiepocalypse). 🧟

If you're feeling stuck with building the body and battling writer's block, remember this:

> YOU CAN'T THINK YOURSELF OUT OF A WRITING BLOCK; YOU HAVE TO WRITE YOURSELF OUT OF A THINKING BLOCK.
>
> — JOHN ROGERS

HORROR SHOW BUILD THE BODY PRO-TIP

At the average speaking rate of 130 words per minute (wpm), a ten-minute speech will have about 1000-1600 words, depending on how fast you speak.

Here's another way to break down the math; the opening and closing typically should be about 10-15% of your speech. That means that the body would be about 70-80%. Looking at it this way, since you only have limited time, don't pack the body with too many points (it's not a voodoo doll). The fewer the main points, the better.

Generally, a 10-minute speech shouldn't have more than 3 points. I know this is a lot of math, but remember, "less is more." Examining the numbers can help keep the content balanced and on topic.

Tell stories:

> MAYBE STORIES ARE JUST DATA WITH A SOUL.
>
> — BRENÉ BROWN

OK, now, let's ditch the numbers and get to the heart of the content, stories.

Humans have been telling stories for thousands of years, and Plato mused, "Those who tell the stories rule society." Although your aspiration may not be to rule society, storytelling is essential to command the stage.

If you struggle with the concept of storytelling, the excellent news is that, essentially, all stories are the same. Whether you're telling your "origin story" or someone else's story, well-told stories follow a similar structure. This structure originated with Joseph Campbell's "Hero's Journey" and has since been adapted into numerous similar formats.

"The Hero's Journey," Joseph Campbell

My favorite adaptation of The Hero's Journey is from Emma Coates, a former storyboard artist at Pixar. She noticed how the structure of all Pixar and Disney movies followed the same template to create compelling stories and box office successes. The framework doesn't work exclusively for fictional storytelling. You can follow it to build your outline, craft persuasive marketing stories, brand narratives, and other content.

You may remember "Mad Libs" as a child. They were a classic road trip time killer where you fill in the blanks of a story with either a noun, adjective, or verb to create surprising outcomes. It's the perfect formula to get started.

This framework is similar in that you are simply filling in the blanks after the prompt.

Let's give it a go. ✍️

Super Easy-Peasy Storytelling Framework

With one of your key messages as inspiration, complete the sentences below...

Once there was...

(Keep this short and sweet.)

.   .   .

Every day...

(The "ordinary world," but things aren't quite right. Stakes and risks are introduced here.)

Then one day...

(This is when a change happens, you cross over the threshold from the ordinary world into the extraordinary world.)

Because of that...

(What changes began to happen next? This is where your story builds momentum.)

Because of that...

(Worth repeating. What happened next because of those previous events?)

Until finally...

This is the end of the story arc when the transformation or wisdom (the gifts of the journey) gained is revealed to the audience. Remember, the ending is more impactful when tied back to the beginning to highlight the contrast.

Example, My Origin Story:

Once I was a little girl who was too scared to speak.

Every day I felt ashamed of my stutter. I tried to hide it from people, which was exhausting. I began to resent myself and develop social anxiety and a paralyzing fear of being asked a question as simple as "What's your name?"

Then one day, as an adult, during a staff meeting, the anxiety of introducing myself led to a near-nervous breakdown.

Because of that, I knew I had to make a change.

Because of that, I faced what I feared most and got up on stage in a storytelling competition and told my story.

Until finally, I realized that if I could overcome my speaking fears, find my voice, and tell my story, I could help others too.

Depending on who your audience is and how much time you have, you can play around with the elements and length of your story. Still, the essential framework and arc remain the same.

I invite you to use this framework to help you get started, and remember to enjoy the process as it evolves and takes root.

What I do know is this; telling stories has a magical quality. And if you believe in magic, tell stories. I double dare you. 🐝

Step Five: Close Strong

Like the opening, closing your speech is an opportunity not to be wasted. I cringe when I hear a speaker give a great speech only to say at the end, "Well, that's all I got, thanks." Be clear, concise, and confident with your final words; leave them wanting more. Because the closing drives home the message and intention of what you wanted your audience to think, feel or do. If you want them to "do" something, be sure your conclusion has a solid call to action.

Bonus points if you link your closing back to the opening. One way to do that is to say the exact quote or question as in the beginning, but with a twist. For instance, when I opened my speech with Rumi's quote, "What you seek is seeking you," I closed my thoughts with, "Now, have you found what you're seeking? Or is it still seeking you?"

If you used a story or a fact to open, you can call back to it in a way that again emphasizes your key message.

And finally, because you always want to end strong, if you include time for questions at the end, prepare a second closing statement or ad-lib based on the questions asked. The point is the last words are important because they become the final thoughts in your audience's mind.

Let them be yours.

Step Six: Rewrite and Rehearse

Rewrite:

Now that you've got your speech written out, outlined, or storyboarded (excellent work, by the way 👋), it's time to rewrite/edit. One way I like to edit is to read the speech out loud. That way, you can hear/see what sounds unnatural, redundant, or grammatically incorrect. Running your written presentation through a program like Grammarly can catch errors and improve clarity and tone. For those who resist editing, GET OVER IT because here's a terrifying guideline; every minute of speech should take one hour of editing. That means you should plan on TEN HOURS 💀 of editing for a ten-minute speech. Oh, the horrors! But seriously, if you want a good speech, extensive editing is unavoidable, like death and... no that's it, just DEATH. 💀

HORROR SHOW ~~EDITTING~~ EDITING PRO-TIP

Make the THESAURUS your best friend you never knew you needed. But trust me, you do. Changing up over-used words elevates your speech and shows that you took extra time and effort and that you genuinely care about your audience... awwww. ✉️

Rehearse:

Once you have a final draft, it's time to rehearse, then rehearse more, and finally, rehearse again.

For those thinking you don't have the time, look at it this way, the key to rehearsing is not to overthink it. You don't need to put pressure on yourself or block hours off your day. Rehearse your speech during all the in-between moments of your day, like when you're doing the dishes, showering, walking the dog, driving, or digging a grave (just making sure you're paying attention, people). These are ideal times because we tend to put less pressure on ourselves when already engaged in another activity. And you'll still be able to internalize your speech.

The goal is to know your speech so well you can be flexible with your words and allow for spontaneity and fun! Remember, FUN?... Right?

Begin with your edited draft, then work your way to rehearsing from only an outline. Next, rehearse your speech from the first word of each section. Finally, to test yourself (for FUN), see how much you can remember by ditching your script altogether.

As you rehearse, notice the parts that seem to drag or sound out of place. Those are the sections that'll need to be reworked or eliminated. Once you're feeling more confident with it, offer to rehearse it for a trusted friend to see if they laugh at the funny parts and cry at the sad parts, not vice versa. You can also try recording yourself in Zoom and watching it back, remembering that you're likely your harshest critic, so go easy on yourself. But watching yourself back is a valuable way to evaluate the effectiveness of your speech.

Think of your speech as a conversation rather than a presentation.

And when having a conversation, everything is natural and carefree.

HORROR SHOW REHEARSING PRO-TIP

As you rehearse, when you find yourself blanking out or forgetting words or lines, don't start over from the beginning. Instead, work through it to practice speaking off the cuff. This way, you'll build confidence that you have the ability and skills on the day of to remain calm, clear and not lose momentum. Don't forget when you need to change things up; your audience won't know the difference unless you tell them, so again, don't ever tell them.

The more you rewrite and rehearse, the more refined your speech will be. And when you can stop worrying about what words are next and instead focus on feeling the emotion of your words and being present, you'll kill it! 🎉

Step Seven: Power of the Pause

I stood under the spotlight before a packed audience at a storytelling championship. As I began, the audience laughed at the funny parts and was attentive to the serious parts. Suddenly, my mind went blank. The room seemed to melt around me. I had forgotten what came next in my story and how to speak. Time froze. After what seemed like a very uncomfortable, slow, and painful death on stage, I remembered where I was, who

I was, and what to say next, and I eventually reached the end. I remember feeling embarrassed and didn't want to speak to anyone afterward. But when it came time to announce the winner, to my disbelief, I heard my name. 😩

The crazy thing was a few of my friends told me later that they thought the long pause in the middle of my speech was one of the most powerful parts! I was like, "Um, yeah, totally planned that, lol!"

What had felt like an eternity to me was only seconds to the audience and added a dramatic pause, ultimately making the story more engaging and suspenseful even though no one was in more suspense than me!

The pause is an underrated and underused tool in our speaker toolbox. When applied for dramatic effect - before and after key points and moments, it can take your speech to the next level.

Pausing also allows the audience to catch up, process, and absorb. Pausing will enable them to silently connect, regroup, or prepare for the next segment.

Now, if you're like most people, you may speak faster when nervous. Especially when we're speaking publicly and are feeling uneasy, our brains tell us if we can get to the end, our pain will cease. So, we rush towards that finish line. 🏃

But if the point is to "get through it" and "get it over with," then why do it?

If it's worth telling, then it's worth pausing. It's worth slowing down. It's worth being present. ⌛

The distance *between* words holds magic too. ╱

That's fantastic, Laura, but how long do I pause?

Typically, when you ask a question, even if it's rhetorical and depending on the question, you'll want to pause long enough for your audience to answer it in their minds. You'll only need to pause for a second or two if it's a yes or no question. But if it's a more profound question like, "What's your favorite childhood memory?" 🌚🌝 the audience needs time to sort through their gazillion memories and pick one; that's gonna take...

(Cue the theme from Jeopardy♪♫) ⏱⏱⏱⏱ LONGER.

Here's why that matters, just like in a real conversation, you never want your audience to wonder, "Why did you even ask a question if you won't allow me time to think about it?" The pause should be long enough for the audience to answer in their mind before you move on to the next point. Otherwise, that's the quickest way to lose your audience's trust. And you always want to maintain your audience's trust.

Add in pauses before and after key points and dramatic parts of your stories for extra impact.

If your audience is laughing, let them! Never interrupt laughing! Perfect pausing demands your attention and being fully present.

Pausing also allows YOU to take a moment, breathe, gather your thoughts, make eye contact. That's a gift for you, too.

Learning to pause is more of a sense than a science, but as you begin practicing, you'll develop it. For example, eventually, pausing will feel more like a couple of heart-beats than a couple of seconds.

 LISTEN TO SILENCE, IT HAS SO MUCH TO SAY.

— RUMI

HORROR SHOW PAUSING PRO-TIP

Write your pauses into your speech. Write the word "PAUSE" and highlight it so that when you practice your delivery, you'll also practice your pauses.

SECRET SIX

FIND DELIGHT IN DARKNESS

" DON'T TAKE LIFE TOO SERIOUSLY, YOU'LL NEVER GET OUT OF IT ALIVE.

— ELBERT HUBBARD

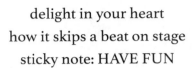

delight in your heart
how it skips a beat on stage
sticky note: HAVE FUN

> WE MUST RISK DELIGHT. WE CAN DO
> WITHOUT PLEASURE, BUT NOT DELIGHT. NOT
> ENJOYMENT. WE MUST ACCEPT OUR GLADNESS
> IN THE RUTHLESS FURNACE OF THIS WORLD.
>
> — JACK GILBERT, *REFUSING HEAVEN*

Happiness Vs. Delight Deathmatch

*W*hat this book is encouraging is not happiness. It's not that I don't want you to be happy. I do! But I invite you to go deeper. I invite you to "risk delight."

Delight sounds similar to happiness, but it's different; delight challenges us. As Webster defines it, "To delight is to take great joy in." Imagine if you took great joy in public speaking. What if you experienced delight every time you stepped onto the stage? When you combine delight with delivering a meaningful message and story, you no longer have to strive to be confident and authentic. You'll be fulfilling your purpose... at least for that audience, on that day.

Are you ready and willing to take that risk? It's like having a happiness vs. delight deathmatch. ⚔

The Two Most Important Words

I took a chance during one of my recent stand-up comedy sets. I decided to talk about suicide, divorce, and depression, you know, funny topics. (It's the example I used in Secret Five) I wasn't sure how the audience would react, but I knew this: as long as I was having fun, the audience would likely have fun too. It became one of my favorite sets because I was deeply connected to my message, and finding humor in life's painful experiences is what the world needs more of.

And there you have it, the two most important words to remember as a speaker: HAVE FUN.

If it seems simplistic, that's because it is. But when it comes down to it, as speakers, we're also creators of experiences for our audience. If we're feeling uncomfortable and nervous, they'll likely feel uncomfortable too. If we're risking delight, they may also take that risk.

The question is, what experience do you want your audience to have?

But My Topic is Very Serious?

Oh, I see. Serious. Ok then, I get you. Here's the thing, no matter how serious or dark your topic is, you can still approach it with joy and add humor. The more serious your subject, the more critical it is to add moments of relief and fun.

One of the best talks I've seen was by a woman who began with a story of finding out she had cancer. Then, one day, while riding her bike on her way home from chemotherapy, she was hit by a car. It was a dark story, but she had the audience cracking up. Although she shared traumatic experiences from her life, she was clearly *risking delight*. Even after over ten years, her talk stands out because of the mix of storytelling, humor, and an important message on the power of perception.

Find humor

To find humor, you must also know your audience well enough to understand what they might find funny. You can also find something relatable to poke fun at, like a shared experience on a small or large scale.

For example, list some challenges you share with the audience. Does everyone in your office share the same disdain for the copy machine? Do you all live some-where experiencing something unique, be it simply a brutally cold winter or maybe, like where I live, a volcanic eruption? Do you have an amusing story of how one of those challenges went wrong? Nothing is as relatable as simply being human and messing up. If we can tell those stories in a way that makes others laugh along with you, it will make for a very memorable part of your speech.

Another way to add humor is to be self-deprecating and honest. If you had a terrible morning leading up to your talk, add a little story about how awful it was; humans love to delight in others' misery! Humor works best when it's relatable. The best part about adding in humor is that it allows you to have more enjoyment in your delivery, and again if you are enjoying it, everyone else will too.

If you can make your audience cry 😭 AND laugh, 🤣 you have genuinely killed it!

HORROR SHOW FIND HUMOR PRO-TIP

Write a sticky note that says "Have fun" and post it on your screen if presenting virtually or in your pocket in person. Look at it; Read it; Say it to yourself over and over again; Embody it; "Having fun" is one of the best intentions and reminders you can give yourself before you begin. Because if you're not having fun... your audience probably won't be having fun either.

OMG I'm Freaking Out

 FEAR IS EXCITEMENT WITHOUT BREATH.

— ROBERT HELLER

I watched the Winter Olympics, and a ski jumper was about to launch himself down an impossibly high and unimaginably steep icy ramp. I felt a little queasy watching from my "comfort zone." The reporter asked him, "So, how do you feel?"

How did he FEEL? 😂 Really? He must have felt anxious and nervous as humanly possible! But that's not what he said; he replied confidently, "I'm excited." 😨 And I could tell he meant it, and not only that, it looked like he was having a heck of a lotta fun. He couldn't wait to do something most of us wouldn't dream of! Still, he was excited. He was fulfilling his passion and purpose; he was trained and ready. He was about to give his gift to the world.

Imagine you're about to give a presentation, and a friend asks how you feel about it. How would you answer?

Maybe: "I'm pretty nervous!" "OMG, I'm freaking out!"

or "I think I might die."

Well, the good news is it's improbable you'll die. (Although possible.) 😄

Here's the kicker, I don't know about you, but when I tell myself I'm excited and going to have fun (or don't like Nutella), my brain seems to believe it. Crazy, right? Because I LOVE Nutella! Our brains are somehow both miraculous and easily tricked.

So, remember that our words are powerful, and our bodies listen to them. When we say to ourselves we're nervous, we suddenly *become* nervous. And by contrast, when we say we're excited, we *become* excited. So which feeling would you choose?

But in some ways, nerves are good. If you're nervous, it means you care. And there's a lot of positive energy when you genuinely care. What if you transformed that energy source into a higher vibration. When I say "higher vibration," I mean the energy that doesn't weigh you down but instead lifts you up.

How do you feel when you give someone a genuine gift from your heart? Are you scared? Are you worried? Are you nervous?

Or do you feel excited? Joy? Grateful? Are you having FUN?

Every time you speak, imagine giving your audience a

gift. And the cool thing is you get to see your audience unwrap it!

Nervousness and excitement are like competitive siblings - they share much of the same DNA and are closely related. 👯

Common symptoms of nervousness include:

- Rapid heartbeat

- Adrenaline rush, sweaty palms, shaking

- "Butterflies" in your stomach

Common symptoms of excitement:

- Rapid heartbeat

- Adrenaline rush, sweaty palms, shaking

- "Butterflies" in your stomach

Hmmmmmmmmm.

This one's a super simple fix!

The next time you feel nervous before speaking, tell yourself you're excited and see how that impacts your performance.

Seriously though, if you're having difficulty believing it... repeat the following to yourself. (With Gusto)

• I'm EXCITED to share my message!

• I'm EXCITED to speak from my heart!

• I'm EXCITED to have fun!

• I'm EXCITED to tell stories!

So, if you want to BE a confident speaker, ask yourself, "How would a confident speaker feel? Would they be excited? Would they risk delight? What would they be doing? A confident speaker would be excitedly submitting proposals to speak at conferences on topics they can't wait to present! They'd work on new ideas and speeches, refining their message and honing their skills. They'd be watching numerous speeches and talks and taking notes on what they want to emulate in different speakers and what they notice could be better. They would learn from every opportunity. And most of all, confident speakers believe in themselves, their message, their story, and their voice.

So, the next time someone asks you how you feel about your upcoming talk, you can say, "I'm excited!"

And eventually, you'll even believe it.

SECRET SEVEN
MOTIVATED BY THE MORGUE

> LIVE BEFORE YOU DIE, SO THAT DEATH IS ALSO
> A LIVELY CELEBRATION.
>
> — B.K.S. LYENGAR

~

imagine the end
don't wait until then, to live
step onto the stage

~

For better or worse, and when I say that, I mostly mean worse; I've had a lot of step-parents. My parents loved each other deeply, but when their marriage ended, they both had numerous failed attempts at new partners. I still recall one of my cousins joking when he couldn't make it to my dad's wedding, "Sorry I can't make it but don't worry, I'll make the next one." 😂

Phyllis became my stepmother in my early thirties, and I was reluctant to let her into my life because histori-cally, for me, stepparents didn't work out so well. But, she proved to be the one exception. Phyllis was born in Cassville, Missouri, and despite growing up very poor, she worked through school and eventually landed at Carnegie Hall. She was funny, elegant, and incredibly generous; she played the harp, of all things.

Phyllis was like a literal angel. 😇

She seemed to have everything, but I learned there was one exception, Phyllis never had any children. And then she got me, a reluctant, standoffish, unappreciative adult for a daughter. But that never stopped her from showing me love, generosity, and kindness. And just when I finally realized how much I wanted her to be in my life, her health suddenly turned for the worse. She had always been physically fit. She walked to work every day and avoided carbs long before that was a thing. Then one day, she was walking to work and noticed that her legs were giving out. She progressively became weaker. It took the doctors a while to figure out what was wrong; when they did, it was a fatal diagnosis. Phyllis died less than two years later of ALS, also known as Lou Gehrig's Disease. She was only fifty-nine.

I'm sharing this with you because it's a reminder that no matter how healthy we are, death comes when it comes. I'm also sharing because, well, ***here's the story...***

I sat in the wooden pew in a packed New York City church. I wore a black lace dress and extremely uncomfortable black heels. But my feet had nothing on the extreme uncomfortableness I felt in my gut.

There was an opening prayer, my dad gave the eulogy, and we sang some of Phyllis's favorite hymns. Then a pastor asked, "Would anyone like to share a story about how Phyllis impacted your life?"

I repeated his words as if they were a command I must obey; "*Share a story about how Phyllis impacted your life.*"

But still, I sat.

I thought back to the time when I returned home after two years in the Peace Corps and automatically went back to waitressing; Phyllis was the one who sat me down and helped me craft my first resume. Because of that, I landed a job in Washington, DC, at Peace Corps Headquarters, leading to others that launched my professional career. Phyllis was the one who helped me set goals and held me accountable.

I watched as a parade of people shared heartfelt stories one after another.

But still, I sat.

But the words I desperately wanted to share with everyone were clear in my mind, they were few, but I felt as if they had already been spoken or etched on my heart:

When I first met Phyllis, I saw her as another unwanted stepparent. But damn if she didn't win me over quickly. I'll never forget December 23rd, 2000, for two reasons. Not only because that was the day my dad and Phyllis got married, at

Carnegie Hall no less, and since it was Christmas time, everything was extra magical, but what IMPACTED me the most were Phyllis's words, "This is my daughter." It was the first time she had introduced me that way. I remember her smile and her look of pride and joy. I smiled back, tears welling up in my eyes because that moment had taken too long to happen. Phyllis was using a cane by then, and I knew our time as mother and daughter was coming to an end.

I don't know if I ever thanked her for the hundreds of ways she positively impacted my life, but I will now. Thank you... Mom.

Me with Dad and Phyllis on their wedding
day.

Phyllis would have been proud of me for sharing it. It would've made my dad proud too. It would've been the best way to honor her and what she meant to me.

But still, I sat.

I'd make a different choice today. I would've stood up. I would've spoken up. But life doesn't work that way.

Soon after Phyllis passed, I realized I only had a limited time to find my voice; I never again wanted to sit quietly at the funeral of someone I loved deeply. But then I took it deeper. I also didn't want to be on my deathbed filled with regret about all the words I never spoke.

That image of me on my deathbed, not as a 100-year-old woman, but as someone at the height of their career, life, and vitality, like Phyllis, motivated me never to sit quietly again.

And if you can take that idea and run even farther into the cemetery with it, imagine this - what if every time you get the opportunity to speak, you speak as if you might die tomorrow? Imagine how that would change how you show up.

"Yes" is perhaps the most beautiful word in English, especially when we say yes to our voice.

> Do you have the courage? Do you have the courage to bring forth this work? The treasures that are hidden inside you are hoping you will say yes.
>
> — JACK GILBERT

Contemplate Your Death

The thing about being alive is that it's easy to forget that one day we won't be.

Take today, for example.

Did you happen to contemplate your death?

Have you considered what it might feel like to be on your deathbed? Or even what friends and family might say at your funeral? Did you wonder who the unlucky soul would be to deliver your eulogy? Hopefully, you got them a copy of this book! 😉

It's funny that on a day-to-day basis, death looks pretty abstract. And when we do think of ourselves dying, we may only picture a much older version of ourselves. It may simply be too disturbing to imagine yourself any younger.

And yet, in every moment, there is a possibility of taking your last breath. One needs only to read the obituaries to know that the Grim Reaper often comes without calling or even sending a quick text first. And that is entirely out of your control. But there is something that IS always in your possession.

I Am Courageous

Courage is not something that you ever need to go looking for. And courage is available to you in every moment. Remember the cowardly lion in The Wizard of Oz? He had courage all along, and you don't have to fight the terrifying flying monkeys to figure that out. Know it to be true. Write it down and remind yourself daily:

I am courageous.

It isn't always self-doubt that gets in our way, though. Sometimes it's simply a lack of motivation. And it's a short trip from the land of self-doubt to the land of "MAYBE SOMEDAY."

Here's the thing, self-doubt often manifests as **procrastination.**

The most clever thing is that, by all accounts, you appear to be busy and getting stuff done. It's the go-to self-sabotage tool. And it works to keep you away from your creative dreams effectively.

I call it "productive procrastination." 😈

The mind loves busy work when avoiding the REAL work needed to break free from your fear.

Your inner critic will tell you with zero irony that you are crushing it. But you are meant to do more than pay bills and fold laundry. You are here to inspire and change lives.

I Have The Courage Now

I was recently asked to give what will likely be one of the most meaningful speeches of my life, a eulogy for one of my best friends. I couldn't help but think back to sitting in the church pew and missing that opportunity with Phyllis. I wasn't ever going to let that happen again. What made it even more special was that my friend, Bree, got to ask me while she was still alive. It was clear she wouldn't be around much longer, and as the true director and producer she was, she spent much of her final days orchestrating and planning her funeral... there would be significant amounts of champagne and cookies. After she asked me, I went home and began writing, hoping to share it with her before she passed. I'll never forget how wonderful it was to read it to her and a small group of her closest friends. She laughed at the funny parts and cried at the heartfelt parts. She looked at me when I finished and whispered, "Thank you."

She died on May 1st, 2023. On June 28th, the day of her memorial service, I stood up and gave my speech to honor Bree to an audience of hundreds. I stood up.

"Give yourself grace to know when to hold
on and when it's time to peacefully let go."

I might not have had the courage to speak at my stepmother Phyllis's funeral years ago, but I have the
courage now to speak for my friend. Some speeches
mean more to us than others, but they all hold the
potential to bring joy, to inspire, and to ultimately
change lives. 🙏

To my dear friend Bree: Cheers to a life of no
regrets. 🥂

FIND WHAT YOU LOVE AND LET IT KILL YOU.

— CHARLES BUKOWSKI

Have No Regrets

Try this visualization when you need more motivation when crafting and working on your speech or presentation.

Take a moment to visualize yourself on your deathbed. You only have a short time left to live, and you're looking back on your life. What's the one hard-won wisdom you've earned when considering your topic? Somehow... share that.

Here's the extraordinary thing about this moment, you have no regrets. You are filled with joy and peace because you've overcome fear, spoken when inspired, and changed lives for the better. Your legacy is etched with moments of courage. Breathe into the feeling of complete satisfaction and peace.

You can picture yourself on your deathbed whenever you feel less than motivated when you notice self-doubt settling in and manifesting as procrastination.

Now, the next time right before you speak, imagine it might be the last, then smile, knowing that you'll show up as you've never shown up before! You'll be present, powerful, and proud of every word! You will NOT be perfect, but you WILL be authentic.

> PEOPLE LIVING DEEPLY HAVE NO FEAR OF DEATH.
>
> — ANAÏS NIN

∼

It's a breezy, clear summer day as I complete my final revisions of this book. My cat is asleep on my (comfort zone) couch beside me, seemingly oblivious to this momentous moment. The birds singing outside are also oblivious; everything is oblivious to the importance and meaning I now hold. Isn't that how life is? We alone create meaning for ourselves. I can't give you meaning; I don't know who "you" are. But I can imagine.

And right now, I imagine you getting to the end of this book and smiling because you feel a bit more courageous than when you began. You have more clarity on how to tell your story and reach your speaking goals. You know that the time leading up for you to speak, whether it's a week, a day, an hour, or a minute, will always hold more fear than when you are in the act of doing it.

You understand that all your fears are there for a reason, and they point you toward liberation from what has been holding you back. I imagine you, and I'm smiling, too, because I know that I didn't write this book for me. I wrote it for you. Thank you for trusting in me and these words, and now it is with all my heart I say, be true to yourself, and you'll surely change lives, even your own.

Live a great story, throw in a plot twist,

L. 🌿

The end. 👻

POST MORTEM

❧

backwards from the end
a new beginning awaits
live a storied life.

❧

W hen my son, Riley, was five, I asked him
a question rarely asked of children. It's a
misconception, the assumption that just because children have not lived as long as adults, they don't have
equal wisdom. I believe that quite the opposite is true.
Yet, as children grow up into adults, they sadly unlearn
most of the innate knowledge they were born with.
Sometimes we remember a glint of it - that wonder-
ment we once had, the delight in living every pure and
precious moment, the secrets of love and joy.

Because I had a young son, I could gain some of the
insight I had lost by asking him questions occasionally.
His answer changed me forever. "What is the meaning
of life?" I asked. He barely looked up at me; he
answered as quickly as if I'd asked if he'd like milk or
juice in his sippy cup. "The meaning of life is to experience life." He said.

Since that moment, I remember that whenever I feel

more lost and unsure of a decision. Can you experience life without leaving your seat? I believe you can.

Me and my shadow taking the stage.

Genuinely experiencing life doesn't have to mean becoming a world traveler and speaking on international stages. If that is your goal, then that's wonderful. But I'd like to leave you with the challenge to simply experience life in each moment.

Feel the rain on your face before you wipe it away, notice how your clothes feel against your skin, your breath sucks in a little deeper when you're relaxed, and you hear your voice. Be so in every moment that it's IMPOSSIBLE to let any of it slip away. You're alive until you aren't. Don't waste your breaths.

Public speaking may be a horror show, but it's also thrilling. *So go on now... kill it... and remember to bring your shadow, because it's with you...*

 ... FOREVER... AND EVER... AND EVER...

— THE TWINS, *THE SHINING*

GRATITUDE

" LET US BE GRATEFUL FOR THE PEOPLE WHO MAKE US HAPPY; THEY ARE THE CHARMING GARDENERS WHO MAKE OUR SOULS BLOSSOM.

— MARCEL PROUST

*T*here are many "charming gardeners" who made this book finally bloom. Some were more like fertilizer, 💩 🌱 others sunshine and rain, but all were necessary, and I'm forever grateful. 🙏

👄 First and foremost, thank you, Cain, for your incredible above and beyond support. ~~You are da bestest~~ You're the best editor ever. 🥰 I **could've** done it without you, but it **wouldn't** have been this good... not even close. But here's the thing, 😉 you have a gift of making EVERYTHING better; this book, my speeches, my life... me. Look how far we've come... and I know it's only the beginning. I love you always, and I love you more. 😜

🌻 To Verity, thank you for saying yes. You were the first person I shared this book with, and I was terrified. But your quick, positive, and moving response means more to me than I can express. From the moment I first heard your story, and met you on our podcast, I knew you were the right person to ask. You wrote the best foreword I could've imagined. 🤍

🍀 To Riley, thank you, you make me want to be a better person, so I can be a better mom, and that's made my life 100 percent better... all because you're in it. I know the past years have been weird and sometimes shitty, but also full of growth. Thank you for sticking by me, loving me, and encouraging me through it all. Don't forget to say "Hi Maui!" on your way home. 🗼 #momcringe.

🪷Thank you to the monster living in my throat 👹. If it wasn't for you, this book wouldn't have been written. You challenged me to fight and work hard for my voice, and that made it even stronger.

🌷 Thank you Mom, for teaching me to "let my heart open, like a rose, so that even in pain it may never close." Falling asleep to the sound of your typewriter was the best lullaby.

🌼 Thank you Dad, for showing me how to live a life full of art, creativity, enthusiasm, and passion... you live in my heart, and I know you're proud.

🐲 To My Vlads, thank you for being my family. You're the best-unexpected brothers ever. I love you both endlessly. Thank you for accepting my first speaking proposal and a few years later, my heart. Our dragon-flies will keep uniting.

🌸 Thank you Audrey, for being the best-bestie-soul-sista ever. Thank you for all the ass kicks and love notes that made this book happen, and all the times you still check in to make sure I'm OK. I love sharing my life, tears, and laughter with you. Even when you make me do stuff I don't want to, like leave the house. I love you always. We're crushing our dreams, together.

❀ Thank you Arliss, for helping me push towards my goals. And for showing me what's possible, by your example, when I get to help someone find their voice.

☘ Thank you Bree; sitting next to you that Thanksgiving day was the luckiest moment in my life! You've inspired me to be courageous and own the confidence you saw in me. We'll toast again one day on that beautiful stage beyond.

🌿 And lastly, thank you to all the readers, especially past "The Backstory Podcast with Cain & Laura" guests, for your positive reviews, "raves" I've included in the book, and helping make it a bestseller, and the world a little more full of inspiring voices and stories. 🙏✨

And THAT'S how you manifest sh*t. 🦄

Xo, L 🌿

LAURA Reid

KEYNOTE SPEAKER
TRAINER
PUBLIC SPEAKING
COACH
STAND UP COMIC
AUTHOR

YOU'VE READ THE BOOK... NOW BOOK LAURA!

SPEAKING & TRAINING TOPICS

- Slay Your Presentations
- Storytelling for Business
- Network with Confidence

SPEAKING AWARDS

5x 1st place winner, 1x Championship winner, Storytelling Competition, New York, 2012-15

1st Place, International Humorous Speech Festival, Hawaii, 2020

Voted "BEST PRESENTATION" International Women's Leadership and Empowerment Conference, Bali, 2020

Toastmasters International Speech Contest, Club, Area, & Division 1st place 2020, 2021, 2022
3rd place District 2020 & 2nd place District, 2022

LET'S CONNECT

laura@thespeechslayer.com
www.thespeechslayer.com

LAURA REID
SPEECH SLAYER

WHY
Laura?

Laura is without a doubt, one of the most extraordinary speakers I have ever encountered. Her ability to inspire and transport her audience through the art of storytelling is truly unparalleled. Her impact is both immediate and lasting, making her an invaluable asset to any speaking engagement.

~Vladimir Mladjenović, Founder & CEO, Tomorrow People

Laura Reid speaks from her heart and soul into the hearts and souls of her audience. With stories and humor, she takes you on a journey of self-discovery. Laura slays the stage and empowers her audience to become the heroes they are.

~Arliss Dudley-Cash, Business Coach & Consultant, Soullutions, LLC.

A wonderful speaker, easy to listen to, time flies by in Laura's workshops. Laura offers solid, applicable tools that are easily implemented. If given the opportunity to learn from her, take advantage of it! You will be glad you did!

~Marty Kennedy, Hawaii Small Business Development Center

Laura's changing the world one story at a time! Her unique approach to story marketing allows participants to go deeply into their stories quickly and thoroughly.

~Aesha Shapiro, Founder, Launch Your Fempire

Laura's approachable poise and relatable humor make her a captivating Speaker. She also has a rare talent for being able to guide others to finding and articulating their own stories with authenticity. If given the chance to have her speak for your event or receive coaching or instruction from her- TAKE IT!

~Ilana Maxwell, Visual Storyteller

With a soothing yet powerful voice, Laura invites you to explore the whole of who you are, and where you want to go next! What I love most about Laura, it doesn't matter if it is a business setting or more casual, she is able to relate to her audiences in a dynamic and captivating way. I would HIGHLY recommend her for any speaking event.

~Lynn Howard, Entrepreneurial Development Strategist

Made in the USA
Columbia, SC
16 October 2024

44486992R00104